Woodwork for the Home

WOODWORK
FOR THE HOME

Mike Lawrence

The Crowood Press

First published in 1991 by
The Crowood Press Ltd
Ramsbury, Marlborough
Wiltshire SN8 2HR

New edition 2001

© The Crowood Press Ltd 1991

All rights reserved. No part of this publication may be reproduced or transmitted in any form or by any means, electronic or mechanical, including photocopy, recording, or any information storage and retrieval system, without permission in writing from the publishers.

British Library Cataloguing-in-Publication Data
A catalogue record for this book is available from the British Library.

ISBN 1 86126 463 1

Acknowledgements

Line drawings by Andrew Green.

The publishers would like to thank the following organisations for supplying the illustrations: Acmetrack (page 49); Black & Decker (pages 12, 13, 14, 16–18); Blue Hawk (page 51); Douglas Kane (pages 31, 84); Dulux (pages 69, 73); Langlow (page 9); Leboff (pages 77, 79); Marley Floors (page 41); Marshall Cavendish (pages 7, 10–12, 57–61, 69, 70, 75, 79, 83, 87, 90, 92, 93); Polycell (page 45); Richard Burbidge (pages 33, 53); Spur (pages 8, 9, 34); Stanley Tools (pages 12–15); Wickes Building Supplies (pages 37, 39, 47, 55, 65, 67, 85); Yale (page 43); 3M (page 92).

Typeset by Acúté, Stroua, G
Printed and bound by Times Ostset (∠na, Malaysia

Contents

Introduction

Wood is one of the most useful materials of all for the do-it-yourself enthusiast, and has been so ever since man first turned to it as a raw material to make tools and utensils. It is readily available, comes in a great many varieties and is easy to fashion into whatever we want to make with it. As a result, in our homes we find ourselves surrounded by wooden things, from furniture and fittings to floors, doors and windows; even the structure of our homes consists of hugh amounts of timber as floor and ceiling joists, roof timbers, and even the house walls themselves in timber-framed houses. We would be lost without it.

Woodworking techniques have, until this century, changed very little since ancient times. Archaeologists have unearthed wooden objects from ancient Egypt assembled with joints we would easily recognize today, and tools from Roman settlements that bear a striking resemblance to their modern counterparts, both in principle and in design. Only in the last few decades have power tools, technological advances such as better adhesives and new products like man-made boards begun to change the way we work with wood, making it easier for even the most ham-fisted amateur to get good results.

This book aims to give you a basic grounding in the use of traditional hand tools and modern powered ones. It shows you how to fix things together with nails, screws, easy-to-use fittings and some of the simpler traditional joints, before taking you on to a series of woodworking projects you may want to carry out in your home . . . or outside it. The indoor projects range from putting up shelves and assembling prefabricated furniture to hanging doors and replacing things like skirtings, architraves and stair handrails. Outdoor projects include replacing windows, putting up a shed, building a porch and erecting fences and gates. All are well within the scope of the average do-it-yourselfer equipped with a modest tool-kit and the confidence to use it.

Working with wood also means keeping what you have in good condition, and in the second part of the book you will find advice on everything from patching rotten woodwork to glazing windows and doing simple furniture repairs. There is also a short chapter on larger-scale woodworking projects which you may prefer to leave to the professional, and finally there is a section that tells you all you need to know about the woodworking materials and sundries you will be using.

THE BASICS

Working with wood is one of the more rewarding aspects of do-it-yourself. The raw material, whether it is natural timber or one of the many man-made boards, is widely available, and it has never been easier to turn it into a wide range of end products around the house – furniture, built-in fittings and features, decorative trims and so on – thanks to manufacturers' efforts to give the woodworker improved tools and accessories to work with. The only limit to what you can achieve is your own skill and ingenuity. Modern adhesives, fillers and finishes mean you can create professional-looking results with ease, and new products such as the ever-growing range of cleverly designed joint fittings make even complex structures easy to design and assemble.

Apart from creating things in wood for use in and around the home, you will also be working with it as part of your home's structure. A typical house contains a surprisingly large amount of wood, in the form of doors, windows, floors, staircases and so on. Any or all of these may need occasional maintenance and repair, and some may warrant complete replacement if wear, neglect or rot have taken their toll over the years.

What to Tackle Indoors

You are likely to want to use wood around the house for a wide variety of projects, even if you are a relative beginner. Here are some of the possibilities.

Shelving Every home needs shelves, ranging from the humblest – for the telephone, perhaps – to grander designs for displaying ornaments or housing books, and surveys show that putting up shelves is the second most common DIY job after interior decorating: over 55 per cent of do-it-yourselfers have tackled it since moving into their present home. It is an area where manufacturers have expended a great deal of effort trying to make life easier for their customers, and you can now buy a wide variety of shelving systems that are child's play to hang and also easy to adjust.

As for the shelves themselves, you can quite literally buy them 'off the shelf'. Veneered or plastic-coated man-made

boards are generally more popular than natural timber planks, although the latter are generally better at carrying heavy loads such as books and records.

Self-assembly furniture Off-the-peg furniture, bought flat-packed ready for home assembly, allows you to install everything from a bedside cabinet to a fully-fitted kitchen. Its main advantage is price; the do-it-yourselfer cannot compete with the major manufacturers when buying materials, so could not make such furniture as cheaply working from scratch. The other big bonus is time-saving; all you have to do is put the items together and, if necessary, fix them to walls and floors. The one drawback is in finding things to fit your home, and here your woodworking skills really come into play; you can either adapt ready-made pieces or build them yourself from scratch. In the latter case you can still save time and effort by incorporating ready-made components such as doors and drawer kits in your designs.

Fig 1 (*above*) A few simple tools and some basic skills are all you need to get started on your woodworking career.

What to Tackle

Home security This may seem an unlikely suggestion for the woodworker to consider, yet installing locks and other security devices involves common woodworking skills such as drilling holes, cutting mortises and housings. With burglary remorselessly increasing year by year, putting better security high on your home improvement agenda could be the most worthwhile step you take for the protection of your home and family. There are easy-to-fit security devices available nowadays for exterior doors (including sliding patio doors), hinged and sliding windows; what is more, fitting them may allow you to qualify for a reduction in your annual household insurance premium.

New door and window furniture Replacing worn, discoloured or broken door furniture – knobs, handles, catches and so on – is well worth considering as part of a general redecoration programme; nothing looks worse than scruffy fittings on gleaming new paintwork. As far as windows are concerned, you can use the opportunity to fit new locking catches and stays and so generally upgrade their security at little extra cost.

New doors Hanging new doors is fast becoming a favourite do-it-yourself job. Fitting a new front door can work wonders in restoring an uninteresting façade (although you need to take care to fit a door in keeping with the style of the house), and gives you the perfect opportunity to improve the door's security too. Replacing interior doors can add the perfect finishing touch to a new colour scheme. Exterior doors now come in a wide range of styles, with both solid and glazed panels, while interior doors are available in plain, panelled and glazed versions in finishes suitable for painting, staining or varnishing, or with exotic wood veneer facings.

Changing the way existing doors hang can also be well worth considering, especially in homes where space is at a premium. Rehanging a door on the other side of its frame so it opens outwards instead of inwards, or changing its hinges from left to right, can often improve access to and from the rooms which the door links, while fitting sliding or folding doors can free valuable floor space, especially for storage cupboards and wardrobes.

New decorative mouldings Another area where new materials can help transform a room is the use of timber mouldings – for example, skirting boards, architraves round door and window openings, and even picture and dado rails (both of which are rapidly coming back into fashion). These are available in a wide range of profiles, including many traditional styles that are ideal for period restoration work, and ingenious fixing techniques now make them easier than ever to install.

New stair parts A timber staircase – even a simple straight flight – is quite a complex piece of joinery, and few do-it-yourselfers will feel able to build or alter one themselves. However, fitting a new balustrade to the stairs and landing is not a difficult job, thanks to the widespread availability of turned balusters and matching handrails, and this can transform the appearance of the staircase, especially if the original has been destroyed or drastically altered by previous owners.

Walls and floors Two other areas of the home which could attract your interest are the walls and floors. Timber cladding provides an attractive, warm and hardwearing finish for walls (and ceilings too),

Fig 2 (*below*) Putting up shelves is one of the most popular of all DIY jobs, and involves only the simplest woodworking skills. Making your own furniture will come later, as your workmanship improves.

especially where existing plastering is in poor condition, while stripping and restoring old timber floorboards can reveal a highly attractive and economical floor surface. For the more advanced carpenter, building timber-framed partition walls allows you the opportunity to reorganize the way you use the floor space within your home – often essential as families grow and the need for separate activity and privacy zones increases.

What to Tackle Outdoors

There is less scope for your woodworking ingenuity outdoors, unless you plan to embark on a programme of building pergolas and gazebos or making your own garden furniture – both areas outside the brief of this book. However, there are several outdoor woodworking projects that are popular do-it-yourself undertakings – and simple to carry out too. These include erecting prefabricated outbuildings such as garden sheds, building simple storm porches using off-the-peg window and door frames, and putting up timber garden fences and gates.

    Replacing windows   This is one major home improvement project which can legitimately be classified as an outdoor job simply because you cannot easily carry it out from indoors. More and more do-it-yourselfers are tackling this job thanks to the growing availability of a wide range of replacement windows of various types.

Maintenance and Repairs

Unfortunately, with so much wood involved in the construction and fitting-out of a typical house, your woodworking skills are likely to be called upon to repair and restore things as well.

    Rot is definitely public enemy number one, especially as far as door and window frames and exterior timber cladding are concerned, and few householders escape having to do battle with it at some time or other. It can also affect interior woodwork, especially timber gound floors if these are not properly ventilated, or any situation where wood remains damp for long periods – as the result of penetrating damp or plumbing leaks, for example. Fortunately, modern preservatives and fillers make light work of tackling the problem.

    Other maintenance and repair jobs you

are likely to have to tackle range from easing sticking doors and windows and replacing broken glass to securing loose floorboards and rickety stair handrails. You may even be called upon to carry out simple repairs to various pieces of furniture – securing loose joints and restoring ill-fitting drawers, for example. They are all dealt with in Chapter 4.

Fig 3 (*above*) Building fitted furniture allows you to tailor-make things to fit your home, and can save you money too.

Fig 4 (*left*) Restoring wooden features in your home to their original glory is an interesting challenge that will develop your skills in renovation and wood finishing.

Raw Materials

The basic raw materials for a wide range of typical woodworking projects fall into two broad groups: natural timber and man-made boards. Natural timber means wood cut from the tree into planks of various sizes and cross-sections, while man-made boards are reconstituted sheet materials made from wood veneers, chippings or fibres. Setting aside the various properties of individual man-made boards for a moment, they all have one huge advantage over natural timber: they come in pieces wider than the widest tree, making them extremely useful for a large range of do-it-yourself projects.

Natural Timber

Botanists divide trees into two types, known as softwoods and hardwoods. The terminology does not mean that the wood is soft or hard; yew, for example, is hard yet is classified as a softwood, while balsa is an extremely soft hardwood.

Softwoods come from coniferous (cone-bearing) trees such as the pine, spruce, larch and fir – all evergreens with needle-like leaves – which grow mainly in a well-defined belt running round the northern hemisphere through Canada, Scandinavia and Siberia. They are the raw material of house-building and the staple fare of the amateur woodworker.

Hardwoods come from broad-leaved deciduous trees – ones that shed their leaves each year – and different species grow all over the world. The group includes European varieties such as ash, beech, elm and oak, and tropical species such as afrormosia, iroko, mahogany, merante, sapele and teak – the so-called tropical rain forest woods being so savagely depleted nowadays. They tend to be much more expensive than softwoods, and the do-it-yourselfer is likely to use them only as trims or in veneered form.

The softwoods are usually subdivided into two groups. The first is commonly called redwood, pine, red deal or yellow deal, while the second is called whitewood, spruce or white deal. Woods in both groups generally have a very pale colour and weak grain pattern, reflecting the speed with which they are plantation-grown nowadays. The wood itself is comparatively strong along the grain direction (though weak across it). It is easy to saw, plane, chisel and sand, and takes screws

well, making it an ideal do-it-yourself material, but it splits if carelessly nailed and is generally not durable enough to be used out of doors unless protected by paint, varnish or a preservative (the one commonly available exception to this last point is Western red cedar).

The hardwoods, by contrast, generally have a deeper colour and more pronounced grain pattern, which is what makes them so attractive to the makers of fine furniture. They vary greatly in strength, durability and ease of working.

Softwood is converted (by sawing) into a wide range of standard sizes. It is important to remember that these are nominal rather than actual sizes; the wood shrinks slightly during seasoning. It may then also be machine-planed, which reduces the actual cross-sectional size still further – by up to 3mm (⅛in) on each dimension for smaller sizes, and more for larger ones. Such timber is described as planed-all-round (PAR), but is still described by its nominal sawn size. Hardwoods are usually sold sawn to similar standard nominal sizes.

Softwoods and hardwoods are also sold machined into a wide range of mouldings for use as decorative trims on furniture, in rooms as skirting boards, door architraves picture rails and the like, and as spindles for balustrades and chair legs.

Fig 5 (*above*) Natural timber – both softwood and hardwood – offers the maximum scope for creativity. Ready-machined mouldings add the finishing touches to many projects.

> **CHECK**
> - that sawn or planed timber is not warped or split, is free from knots (unless you want knotty wood) and is not oozing resin.
> - that man-made boards have undamaged corners and edges, and that veneered or plastic-coated finishes are in good condition.
> *See also* pages 87–9.

Man-Made Boards

Man-made boards can be divided up into four main types: fibreboard, made by compressing wood fibres; chipboard, made by bonding wood chips together using synthetic resins; plywood, consisting of thin wood veneers glued together; and blockboard, which is essentially plywood with a solid timber core.

Hardboard This is the most widely used of the fibreboards. It is relatively weak, and so must be supported by a framework. However, it is cheap and will easily bend round curves.

Medium board This is softer and weaker than hardboard, so is usually used in thicker sheets. Dense types are used for cladding partitions instead of plasterboard, while softer types are used for pinboards.

Medium-density fibreboard (MDF) This is far stronger than other fibreboards because adhesive is added to bind the fibres together, and it is much denser than medium board. It is finding increasingly widespread use in the home.

Chipboard This is a rigid, dense and fairly heavy board. It is strong if reasonably well supported, but sawing can leave a crumbly edge (and the resin content quickly blunts saw blades), and screws do not hold well in it.

Chipboard is also widely available with the board faces and edges covered with natural wood veneers, PVC or melamine coatings, or with plastic laminate.

Plywood This gets its strength and resistance to warping from the fact that the veneers are bonded together with the grain direction at right angles in alternate layers. It is also available with a range of exotic surface veneers in woods such as teak, oak and mahogany, or with a decorative plastic surface finish.

Blockboard This has a thick core consisting of strips of natural timber, sandwiched between outer veneers whose grain runs at right angles to the core grain. It is a relatively dense, strong (and expensive) board, but it can be hard to get the edges neat if the core end grain is exposed and making fixings into this edge of the board can be difficult.

Laminboard This is a high-quality type of blockboard with thinner, more uniform strips forming the core. It is expensive and hard to find, and is used only where the quality justifies the price.

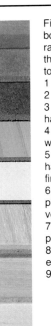
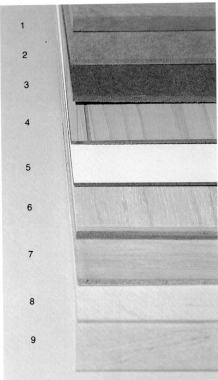

Fig 6 (*left*) Man-made boards come in a wide range of types. Amongst the thinner ones are (from top):
1 12mm medium board;
2 3mm hardboard;
3 6.5mm oil-tempered hardboard;
4 4mm hardboard with woodgrain finish;
5 3.5mm oil-tempered hardboard with melamine finish;
6 15mm stout-heart plywood with pine surface veneers;
7 6mm stout-heart plywood;
8 4mm birch exterior-grade plywood;
9 1.5mm birch plywood.

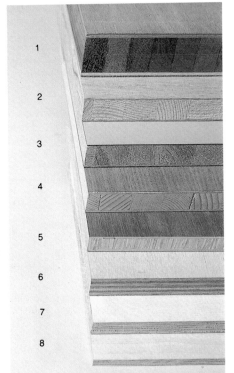

Fig 7 (*left*) Thicker man-made boards include (again from top):
1 veneered blockboard with cedar core, ideal for door blanks;
2 beech-faced blockboard;
3 laminate-faced blockboard;
4 walnut veneered blockboard;
5 mahogany-faced laminboard;
6 thick-core plywood;
7 & 8 exterior-grade plywood.

The Essential Tool-Kit

Even if your woodworking activities are strictly limited, you will not get far or achieve very good results without using the right tools. Here is a guide to help you build up a useful and practical tool-kit without having to spend a fortune.

Basic Fixings

Perhaps the simplest of all DIY jobs involve putting up things like shelves, cupboards and so on. In each case you have to make a fixing of some sort – either by driving in a nail or screw. Masonry nails are in principle easier to use than screws for making wall fixings; all you need to drive them is a hammer. However, it is not always easy to fix them exactly where you want them, and often difficult to get them out again. Screws are better: they provide a more secure grip, and can be undone easily if you want to move or change whatever it is that you have fixed. The only trouble is that you need separate tools to make the hole and drive the screw.

Drill Requirement number one is a drill. These days there is little point in buying a hand drill like grandfather used (although one can be useful for the occasional job if you are working away from a power source). Invest in an **electric drill**, ideally one with a 13mm (½in) chuck, variable speed control and hammer action, so you can tackle a wide range of drilling jobs in all sorts of materials with just one tool. See page 16 for more details about drills.

You will also need an extension cable so you can use your drill (or any other power tool, for that matter) further away from a power point than the flex will allow. Buy one with flex rated at 13amps rather than 5amps, so you can use it for running equipment like heaters, when you are not using it for DIY jobs.

For actually making the holes, you need some **drill bits**. Buy high-speed, steel **twist drills** for making holes in wood, plus two or three different-sized **masonry drills** for making holes in walls. Twist drills are usually sized in millimetres or in fractions of an inch; masonry drills are sized by numbers that match screw gauges, or in millimetres. Both types are sold singly or in sets.

Screwdrivers For driving in the screws, you need a **screwdriver**. To be precise,

you need several screwdrivers, because screws come in several sizes and have heads of different types. For the driver to work efficiently, its blade must match the slot or recess in the screw head. If it slips out, it will damage whatever you are fixing. You can probably get by with just two **flat-bladed screwdrivers** of different sizes for driving slotted screws, plus one **cross-point driver** for cross-head screws. (*Pozidriv* and *Supadriv* are the commonest type; a No 2 size screwdriver will drive the most widely-used screw sizes.)

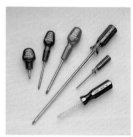

Fig 8 (*above*) A selection of the tools you are likely to need for the jobs and projects in this book.

Fig 9 (*below left*) The one tool you will find it hard to do without is a power drill. Choose a variable speed model.

Fig 10 (*below*) Screwdrivers drive screws. You will need drivers for cross-head screws as well as for traditional slotted-head screws.

The Essential Tool-Kit

Measuring and marking tools   There are a couple of other tools you will find invaluable when you are putting things up. The first is a retractable steel **measuring tape**, to help you get your fixing holes the right distance apart and at the right height. Choose one with a tape at least 3.5m (12ft) long, marked with both metric and imperial measurements; it is a good idea to choose one with a lock so you can take long measurements without the tape retracting unexpectedly. The second tool is a small **spirit level**, invaluable for ensuring that you fix things like shelves to a true horizontal. Choose one about 600mm (2ft) long with a metal body and both horizontal and vertical indicators; then you can use it as a straight-edge too. Add a pencil, so you can mark the positions of screw holes, draw guide lines and so on.

Hammer   Despite what was said earlier about the superiority of screws for making secure fixings, a **hammer** is a tool no home should be without. You need one for simple jobs like driving picture nails, and for all sorts of other tasks like nailing down loose floorboards and mending fences. Choose a **claw hammer**, which can pull nails out as well as drive them.

Sharp knife   There are all sorts of do-it-yourself jobs where a sharp knife is invaluable, and it is far and away the best tool for marking cutting lines on timber. Choose a handyman's knife with a retractable blade, so you can carry it around safely, and buy a selection of blades for it such as ordinary cutting blades, perhaps a laminate cutter, and even a padsaw blade for making small cut-outs in wood and other materials.

Tenon saw   Even if you plan to do no more carpentry than cutting a veneered chipboard shelf to length, you must have a saw. A **tenon saw** will cope with most small sawing jobs on thin boards and on timber up to about 50mm (2in) thick. Choose one with a 300-350mm (12-14in) blade. Invest in a **try-square** too, so you can make sure your saw cuts are absolutely square to the edges of your workpieces. Alternatively, choose a **combination square** – a dual-purpose square that will mark 45° angles for mitres as well as right angles.

If you prefer, buy an **electric jig saw**. This is an extremely versatile tool which can cut straight lines, curves and other intricate cut-outs in a wide variety of materials as well as wood and man-made boards. All you have to do is fit the appropriate type of cutting blade. Choose one with variable speed control, so you can use a low speed for hard materials and a high speed for softer ones like wood and plastic See page 17 for more details.

Rasp   If you are working with or repairing wood, there are likely to be a variety of shaping jobs you will have to tackle. A general-purpose plane/rasp is ideal for working with wood and man-made boards, and can tackle metal and plastic too. They come in a range of styles, including flat rasps, planer-files, round files and block planes. All have replaceable blades.

Junior hacksaw   You are likely to have to tackle some small metal-cutting jobs, especially away from the workbench

See pages 90–3 for more information on screws, nails, wallplugs and other hardware.

Fig 11 (*below left*) Hammers drive nails (and have numerous other unofficial uses). The claw type can pull wayward nails out too.

Fig 12 (*left*) The power jig-saw is a jack of all trades, capable of making both straight and curved cuts in timber and boards.

Fig 13 (*below*) Shaping tools include planes, with blades you have to sharpen on an oilstone, and Surforms which use replaceable blades.

where you could not use a jigsaw even if you had one. A junior hacksaw takes cheap, throw-away blades which are simply snapped into place in the frame.

Portable workbench One of the biggest difficulties facing the DIY beginner is finding somewhere to carry out his or her DIY jobs. A portable workbench is a must. You can take it to wherever you are working and provide a firm, stable surface on which to saw, hammer and drill things to your heart's content. You can also use it as a vice for gripping things as small as a piece of moulding or as large as a door. You can even stand on it and use it as a makeshift working platform for maintenance jobs indoors and out.

Access equipment You obviously do not need access equipment for woodworking itself, but for jobs like fitting shelves and hanging wall units you will need a **step ladder** – ideally with a top platform where you can rest tools and equipment. For maintenance work outdoors you are certain to need an **extension ladder**. Choose a light-weight aluminium one.

Whatever access equipment you are using, keep safety very much in mind; falls from ladders and steps are the third most common cause of domestic accidents. Always secure ladders to the building in some way; do not lean out too far when you are working from them, and take special care as you ascend or descend, especially if you are carrying anything. If you don't like heights, don't climb at all.

Tools for Serious Woodworking

Once you start to take your woodworking seriously by tackling more than just routine fitting and maintenance jobs, you begin to enter the realms of the professional tradesman and you will find that you need a whole host of extra tools to help you to do the job properly. Here is a look at the tools you cannot do without, plus some that make it easier and quicker to get top-quality results.

What tools you need for woodworking projects depends on the answers to two questions. Firstly, will you be tackling general structural carpentry and simple furniture-making only, or are you intent on becoming a master cabinet-maker? Secondly, do you want to use traditional hand tools wherever possible, or to put your faith as much as possible in modern power tools? Your answers will dictate the contents of your tool kit, over and above the essential basic tools described earlier. Throughout this section you will find power tool alternatives to traditional hand tools mentioned where appropriate.

Let us assume you will be just a general-purpose chippie, doing jobs like building stud partition walls, laying floorboards and perhaps making fitted furniture using a lot of man-made boards; this book is not intended for the dedicated craftsman. For general cutting work you will need a **panel saw**, or an **electric jigsaw** or **circular saw** – *see* page 17. A jigsaw will most often be used free-hand, but a circular saw is more versatile if used in conjunction with a **saw table**. For curved cuts you will need a **coping saw**, and for making cut-outs within a workpiece a **padsaw** will be invaluable (a jigsaw can do both these jobs if you prefer power to hand tools).

For reducing wood to the cross-section you require, you will need either a **smoothing plane** or an electric **power planer** – *see* page 18. You can shape it using traditional hand tools such as **rasps** and **spoke-shaves**, or once again let power tools do the work for you; you could use a **belt sander** (page 17) for fast stock removal, plus a range of drill attachments such as **drum sanders** and **rotary wood rasps** to do the finer shaping work.

If you want to create mouldings such as staircase spindles and chair legs from square stock, you will need a **lathe** (page 18) plus a set of woodturning tools. If

Fig 14 (*left*) The portable workbench allows you to work anywhere around the house, and does double duty as a large vice too.

Fig 15 (*below*) Saws come in a wide range of styles and sizes. Shown here are the panel saw, the keyhole or padsaw and a junior hacksaw.

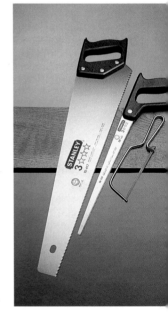

The Essential Tool-Kit

grooving, edge shaping and similar activities appeal to you, a **power router** (page 18) is the perfect answer.

When it comes to cutting joints, recesses for hinges and mortises for locks, a set of **wood chisels** is essential, whether you prefer hand or power tools (although a relative newcomer called the *Powerfile* can be used to cut mortises and other recesses reasonable well). Bevel-edge chisels are more versatile than firmer chisels because you can undercut with them; you need at least four, in 6, 12, 18 and 25mm (¼, ½, ¾ and 1in) widths. Choose plastic handles rather than wooden ones, so you

can drive them with your claw hammer instead of a mallet. You will need an oilstone to keep them sharp.

Talking of hammers, it is worth adding a small **pin hammer** to your tool-kit, for driving small nails, glazing sprigs and the like. A **staple gun** is also useful, since it allows you to fix thin sheet materials with one hand free to position the work while the other fires the staples.

For making holes in wood, the **power drill** mentioned earlier reigns supreme. You can fit drill bits of all sorts into it for making large and small holes, and with a **hole saw attachment** you can cut even larger holes in sheet materials. A **vertical drill stand** is a vital accessory if you do a lot of precision drilling, since it ensures that holes are drilled precisely vertically and, if necessary, to just the right depth. A **dowelling jig** is also well worth buying if you use dowel joints a lot, since it ensures that the dowel holes mate exactly on the adjoining pieces. If you prefer to stick to hand tools, a **hand drill** will tackle

small holes and a **brace and bit** larger ones.

For assembling the fruits of your labours, some **cramps** will be invaluable. There are many different patterns on the market nowadays; add them to your tool-kit as you find you need them. Use your portable workbench as a vice until you can justify buying a woodworker's vice.

A **countersink bit** for your hand or power drill enables you to recess screw heads below the wood surface; a **nail punch** lets you hide nail heads beneath a blob of filler. Lastly, it will pay you to expand your selection of **screwdrivers**, both flat-bladed and cross-point types. If you have a lot of repetitive driving to do, invest in either a **spiral ratchet screwdriver** or a cordless **power screwdriver** (page 16); both come with a range of interchangeable bits.

The last stage in any woodworking project is the final finishing ready for decoration. You can either do this by hand with abrasive paper and a **sanding block**, or invest in a **power orbital sander or finishing sander** — see page 17).

Fig 16 (*left*) Chisels are essential for cutting some joints.

Fig 17 (*below*) You will need cramps for all sorts of assembly jobs.

Fig 18 (*below left*) Hand drills are useful for jobs remote from a power supply.

Fig 19 (*below*) Braces drive larger bits than hand or power drills can accept.

Power Tools

Power tools are here to stay, and many do-it-yourselfers do not even own traditional hand tools like saws and planes any more. There are also several specialist power tools with no precise manual equivalent which can be very useful to have around the workshop. Here is a brief look at what each category of power tool has to offer, and what you should be looking for whether you are buying for the first time or replacing what you've got.

Drills An electric drill will not only drill holes in wood, man-made boards, plastic, metal and masonry; it will also drive a wide range of useful attachments that can save time and effort.

The cheapest type is the **single-speed drill**, usually with a chuck size of 10mm (⅜in) and a maximum drilling diameter of about 19mm (¾in) in wood – ideal for small-scale light-duty drilling work. Larger, more powerful models – generally from 'professional' ranges – are also available, capable of more sustained work without burning out.

Two-speed drills allow you to select a high speed for drilling wood and a low one for metal and masonry, and are generally more versatile than single-speed types. Models are available with 10mm and 13mm (½in) chucks, and drilling capacities are likely to be around 25mm (1in) in wood. Most two-speed drills now have hammer action as well, which makes drilling holes in masonry easier.

Variable-speed drills give you even more flexibility than having two speeds, since you can choose the right speed for the job and vary it while you are working. Most variable-speed drills now have hammer action, and this is the best type to choose for all-round versatility. Most have 13mm (½in) chucks, although some heavy-duty models with 16mm (⅝in) chucks are available in 'professional' ranges.

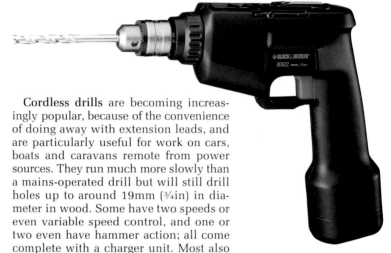

Cordless drills are becoming increasingly popular, because of the convenience of doing away with extension leads, and are particularly useful for work on cars, boats and caravans remote from power sources. They run much more slowly than a mains-operated drill but will still drill holes up to around 19mm (¾in) in diameter in wood. Some have two speeds or even variable speed control, and one or two even have hammer action; all come complete with a charger unit. Most also have reverse gear, making them ideal for driving and removing screws too, although they are rather heavy for this and you may prefer to add a separate cordless screwdriver to your tool-kit instead,

Screwdrivers One of the fastest-selling power tools today is the cordless screwdriver, which has developed from the cordless drill into a compact lightweight unit that can pack a surprising amount of screwdriving power. Basic models have a single speed, with a spindle lock for manual screwdriving and forward and reverse gears. More sophisticated types feature variable torque control to cope with variations in power demand.

Sanders Sanding, especially when large areas are involved, is the perfect job for some powered assistance. Two types of tool are worth having – the orbital sander and the belt sander.

Orbital sanders have a flat rectangular baseplate which is covered with a soft cushion over which a sheet of abrasive paper is fitted. The motor drives the baseplate via an eccentric pin mechanism, giving an orbital scrubbing action at very high speed. Most orbital sanders are either 'third-sheet' or 'half-sheet' models, meaning that the baseplate will accept one-third or one-half of a standard-sized sheet of abrasive measuring 280×230mm (11×9in). There are also a number of smaller models called palm-grip sanders, which take a quarter-sheet of abrasive and are ideal for small areas where a larger

Fig 20 (*above*) Cordless drills pack a surprising amount of power and can be quickly recharged.

Fig 21 (*above*) Cordless screwdrivers are a boon for repetitive screwdriving, and can be used to remove screws too.

Fig 22 (*left*) Power drills not only drill holes; they can also drive various power tool accessories.

tool will not go. Some models have variable speed control, and a growing number feature dust bags or a dust extraction facility via a vacuum cleaner.

Belt sanders use a continuous belt of abrasive that runs round two rollers, and can be used freehand or as a bench-mounted tool. They are a heavier-duty tool than an orbital sander, and can remove more material more quickly. Because they create so much dust, a dust bag or dust extraction facility is essential, and all models offer one or both options. The majority take belts 65 or 75mm (2½ or 3in) wide; larger professional-quality machines take belts 100mm (4in) wide. Again, some models have variable speed control.

A sanding tool with a difference is the unique **Black & Decker Powerfile**. This has a narrow belt of abrasive running round a guide bar – it looks rather like a miniature chain saw – and is useful for a wide range of sanding and shaping jobs on surfaces where a power sander or similar tool cannot reach. There are two models, one with a fixed speed and one with variable speed control.

Jigsaws These saws can carry out all sorts of general-purpose cutting jobs in wood, man-made boards, and also thin metal and plastic sheet materials. They will also do the job of a coping saw or padsaw when making cut-outs away from the edge of the wood, or when cutting curves. Used with a fence or guide batten, they will make long straight cuts, with bevelled edges if the soleplate is tilted.

Single-speed saws have cutting capacities of around 50mm (2in) in softwood – enough for most general-purpose work.

Two-speed saws have a slower second speed setting which can be useful when cutting curves or awkward shapes. They are almost extinct now, their role having been taken over by **variable speed saws**. Motors are generally more powerful than single-speed models and cutting capacity is generally greater too; expect to manage up to 70mm (2¾in) in wood. This type is the best choice for the serious woodworker.

Scrolling saws allow you to rotate the blade assembly as you saw, by turning a large knob on the front of the saw body. This allows you to follow intricate cuts much more accurately, making the saw a powerful competitor to the traditional fretsaw and ideal if you do a lot of craft work. Most are variable-speed models.

Many jigsaws offer additional features such as a retractable soleplate, allowing you to saw right up to obstacles, and either a dust collection bag or a spigot that can be connected to a vacuum cleaner.

Fig 23 The unique Powerfile (*above*) can be used for sanding, shaping and even mortising jobs.

Fig 24 Orbital sanders (*left*) take the hard work out of wood finishing.

Circular saws These are less popular than jigsaws amongst do-it-yourselfers, but for the serious woodworker who likes to prepare his own timber instead of depending on off-the-peg sizes from the local timber yard they are a must. They can be used free-hand or else set up in a saw table for use as a bench saw. Standard features include a tiltable soleplate, allowing bevelled cuts to be made, and an adjustable rip fence to allow cuts to be made parallel to and a fixed distance away from the edge of the workpiece. Some models feature a dust extraction facility, like the jig saws mentioned earlier.

The smallest and cheapest type of saw takes a 125mm (5in) diameter blade and gives a maximum cutting depth of around 30mm (1¼in), reducing to around 22mm (⅞in) for cuts made at an angle of 45°. Models taking 150mm (6in) blades give cutting depths of up to about 45mm (1¾in).

Stepping up to the semi-professional saws, there are models taking blades about 180mm (7⅛in) in diameter and capable of cutting to depths of about 60mm (2⅜in). Most powerful of all are models taking 235mm (9¼in) diameter blades, capable of cutting wood up to 85mm (3⅜in) thick.

Power planers Power planers are similar in outline to an ordinary bench plane, but the cutting action is provided by a rotating drum fitted with two cutting blades and mounted in the centre of the soleplate. Cutting depth is altered by adjusting the soleplate position, and may range from about 0.5mm (less than 1/32in) per pass on smaller models up to around 3mm (⅛in) on more powerful machines. Most have a cutting width of around 82mm (3¼in) – wider than a bench plane.

Routers Power routers are among the most useful and versatile tools for the specialist woodworker, because the range of cutters available makes it possible to cut a huge range of slots, grooves, chamfers, rebates and decorative profiles. The cutter rotates at extremely high speed - around 24,000rpm – and so produces a clean fast cut so long as the cutters are sharp.

Almost all do-it-yourself routers are the plunge-action type, which means that the cutter is plunged down through the soleplate into the workpiece to start the cut.

Specialist tools Lathes are bench-mounted woodturning tools, used mainly by the specialist furniture-maker. An integral tool will be comparatively expensive, but for small-scale work a lathe attachment that can be driven by an electric drill may be an acceptable alternative.

Work centres are portable or fixed power tool stations designed to accept a wide range of tools, allowing them to be used as bench-mounted tools with much greater precision and freedom than free-hand operation allows.

Fig 25 Routers (*above*) cut grooves and edge mouldings, giving a highly professional finish.

> **CHECK**
> • that you know how to operate any power tool before you start work.
> • that drills, blades and router bits are securely fitted to the tool.
> • that safety guards (where fitted) are operating properly.
> • that the flex is in good condition and is securely anchored within the tool body.
> • that you store tools out of the reach of children, and never allow them to use tools unsupervised.

Fig 26 Power planers (*left*) allow you to reduce off-the-shelf wood to non-standard sizes.

Shopping and Safety

You are likely to need quite a range of different materials to carry out the sorts of woodworking projects and repairs covered in this book. Where you shop for them depends on the scale and nature of the job; for a simple repair you may need to look no further than your local hardware store, but for more extensive projects you will make considerable savings by shopping around for materials. Here are the places to try.

Local DIY Shops

The typical independent high street DIY shop usually stocks a basic range of woodworking hand tools (but seldom any power tools; it cannot compete with the prices in the DIY superstores), plus small packs of products like nails, screws, abrasives, adhesives and fillers, hinges and furniture fittings. You will probably be offered a choice of just one or two brands. Some stock softwood, usually in a restricted range of sizes and lengths, and may offer a cut-to-size service for man-made boards.

Verdict Fine for small jobs if the shop has what you need and the convenience outweighs the disadvantage of highish prices. Generally good at offering advice.

DIY Superstores

The major national chains all offer a good range of tools and materials for woodworking projects of all types. Softwood is usually planed and sold in single lengths or in pre-packs of five or ten lengths, and you will find a good stock of softwood and hardwood mouldings too. All also stock the various sheet materials, and some will cut sheets to size for you. Most carry a range of intereior and exterior doors plus all the furniture and security devices needed to fit them. Some stock windows, kitchen units and stairparts (usually in kit form), and stores with garden centres also sell fencing and sheds.

They are also strong on hand and power tools and all the sundries you will need, with several brands to choose from.

Verdict Excellent range of relevant products, usually at average-to-keen prices, but unlikely to offer much in the way of technical advice. Many open late in the evenings, and some on Sundays. Some will deliver bulky goods and will also hire equipment.

Timber Merchants

The obvious place to go for large quantities of softwood, man-made boards and manufactured joinery such as doors, windows, stairparts and kitchen units (although not all stock these). Many also stock tools and woodworking sundries.

Verdict Generally the cheapest for timber products, especially for large-scale projects, but only average for other materials and tools. Not open at weekends.

Builders' Merchants

A good source of supply for replacement doors, windows, security fittings, kitchen units, stairparts, fences and garden sheds, and for large quantities of things like paint, varnish, woodstains and preservatives. Quite a few do not stock 'raw' timber. Some have 'retail' counters designed to cater for the non-trade customer.

Verdict Reasonable selection of goods at average prices, although tools may seem expensive since they generally stock only professional-quality products. Good for large-scale projects. Not open at weekends.

Kitchen Specialists

The best source for kitchen units, although some may carry only their own brand so you may have to shop around for choice. Most offer design and fitting services.

Verdict Fine if you can find the range you want, and good for technical advice. Prices vary widely; choose with care.

Fencing Contractors

The obvious choice for fencing, gates and prefabricated garden buildings. All offer a delivery service, and some will put things up for you too.

Verdict Generally the keenest prices around for what they stock. Some open on Saturdays but not Sundays.

Garden Centres

Some stock fencing, garden gates and sheds, but generally only a restricted range. You may also find a restricted range of tools and sundries.

Verdict Usually on the expensive side for materials, but most will deliver. Many are (legally) open on Sundays.

SAFETY
All tools need handling with care, especially power tools (*see also* page 18). This will ensure that they do their job well, stay in good condition and – most importantly – do not injure you.

• When using bladed tools such as chisels or saws, always ensure that the direction of cut is away from your body. Make sure the blade is sharp.
• When using hammers, ensure that the face of the hammer head strikes the nail squarely. Wear goggles when driving masonry nails.
• When using screwdrivers, make sure you use one with the correctly-sized tip so it does not slip out and damage the workpiece as you drive the screw.
• When using power tools, follow the safety advice given on page 18.

None of the jobs described in this book is inherently dangerous; you are rarely working at heights, or handling heavy or noxious materials. However, it is worth remembering that sawdust can be an irritant to the lungs, so wear a face mask (and possibly safety spectacles) when sanding or power sawing. Wear gloves when handling broken glass.

Cutting Wood by Hand

Perhaps the most basic woodworking skill of all involves cutting wood to length. Many amateur woodworkers are happy to work with planed softwood or planks of man-made board materials bought in standard sizes, designing the projects they carry out to avoid wherever possible the need for cutting material down in width. Indeed, the manufacturers of veneered and plastic-coated boards offer such a wide range of widths and lengths that it is often possible to avoid any cutting at all on simple projects like shelf units.

However, with softwood most commonly sold in 2m or 2.4m (6ft 6in or 8ft) lengths, you have no option but to learn how to cut these long lengths down to the size you require. You can use a hand saw for this (a tenon saw for wood of relatively small cross-section, a panel saw for wider boards), or resort to a power saw if you prefer (see opposite). Whichever you use, remember the cardinal rule of sawing: to cut on the waste side of the cutting line, so that your workpiece does not end up fractionally too short.

What to do

Whether you are using a hand or a power saw, the first step is to measure off the length of wood you want and to mark a cutting line on your workpiece. When cutting to length you want a cut that is square to the edges of the wood. Use your try square to mark this, holding the stock against the edge of the wood and drawing a line along the edge of the blade with a sharp hard pencil or, better still, a handyman's knife. When cutting softwood, repeat the process to mark the cutting line on the adjacent faces of the wood too.

To hold wood of small cross-section steady while you cut it, use a bench hook – either bought or home-made (see TIP). Start the cut carefully with gentle backward strokes of the saw, then complete it with strokes parallel with the bench top.

On wider workpieces, use a panel saw and support the workpiece on a portable workbench if you have one, or on some other makeshift support such as a pair of steps laid on their side.

What you need:
- tape measure
- try square
- pencil or marking knife
- straight-edge
- tenon saw
- bench hook (see below)
- panel saw
- portable workbench

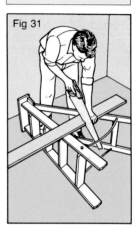

Fig 31

Fig 31 Improvise a saw horse by using things like stepladders to provide support.

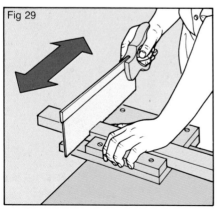

Fig 27

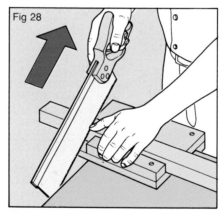

Fig 28

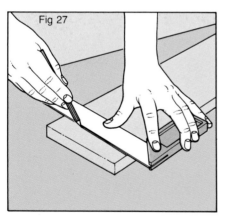

Fig 29

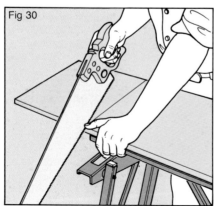

Fig 30

Fig 27 Always use a try square and a pencil or marking knife to mark your cutting lines square to the edge of the workpiece.

Fig 28 Use a tenon saw for cutting timber of small cross-section, plus a bench hook to hold small workpieces on your bench. Start the cut with the saw blade at an angle.

Fig 29 As the cut deepens, bring the saw blade to nearer the horizontal and complete the cut.

Fig 30 Use a panel saw for cutting wider and thicker workpieces.

Using Power Saws

Power tools have become so popular with do-it-yourselfers in recent years that many people have virtually dispensed with hand tools altogether. Sawing is one area where this is particularly true, and the tool concerned is the jigsaw. This has a fairly short, stiff blade which is driven up and down in much the same way as a sewing machine needle, cutting through the wood as the tool is 'driven' along the cutting line. The cheapest saws have a single cutting speed, but more expensive models have variable speed control.

The jigsaw can be used free-hand for short cuts – across the grain of small-section softwood or narrow boards, for example – but for longer cuts it is better to guide the saw body with a guide batten or fence attachment. The maximum cutting depth is around 55mm (just over 2in).

The base of the saw is adjustable, allowing the blade to make angled cuts as well as straight ones, and some models have a scrolling facility, allowing the blade to be turned independently of the saw body for cutting tight curves.

What to do

Fit a blade to the saw to match the material you are cutting (softwood or man-made board, for example) and the finish you want (coarse, medium or fine). Rest the nose of the soleplate on the wood with the edge of the blade aligned with the cutting line but not touching it. Start the saw up and move it forwards so it begins to cut, keeping the soleplate flat on the surface of the wood. Move it steadily forwards without forcing it, making sure the blade does not wander on free hand cuts. Support the offcut as you complete the cut.

For long cuts, either run the saw body along a guide batten cramped to the workpiece, or use a fence attachment. The latter can be used only for cuts fairly close to the wood's edge, due to the length of the fence arm.

To make angled cuts, undo the knob securing the soleplate to the saw body and rotate the plate to the desired angle. Lock it in place and make a test cut on scrap wood before cutting your workpiece.

What you need:
- jig saw
- saw blade
- tape measure
- straight-edge
- pencil *or* marking knife
- guide batten
- G-cramps
- fence attachment
- protractor

CHECK
- that you are using the correct saw blade for the material you are working on.
- that the blade will not cut into your bench or other surface while you are making the cut.
- that you do not force the blade, or it may wander off line.

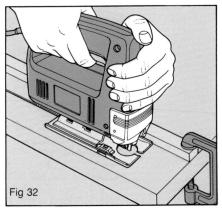

Fig 32

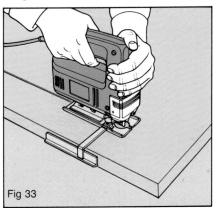

Fig 33

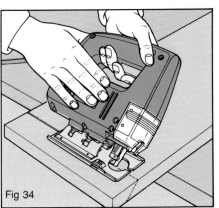

Fig 34

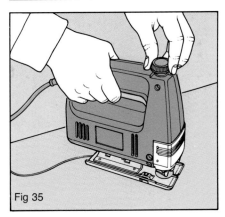

Fig 35

Fig 32 Cramp a batten to your workpiece to guide the saw blade when making straight cuts with a jig saw.

Fig 33 For cuts close to and parallel with the board edge, use a fence to guide the saw.

Fig 34 Tilt the saw blade to make angled cuts such as mitres. Test the cutting angle on scrap wood first.

Fig 35 Do not force the saw when cutting curves, or you will jam and twist it. Use a special scrolling jigsaw for cutting tight curves.

Using Drills

There will be plenty of situations where you will need to drill a hole in the wood you are working on. It may be a clearance hole for a screw, which will split the wood if you try to drive it without one, a series of holes for the dowels that make a dowel joint, or a larger hole to accept the body of a cylinder lock in your front door. For all these jobs you need something to bore the hole, and a tool to drive it. The traditional tools are the hand drill and the carpenter's brace, but both have now been widely supplanted by the mains-powered or cordless electric drill.

The most widely used drilling aid is the steel twist drill, which fits either a hand or a power drill. This is a rod with its tip sharpened to give two opposed bevelled cutting edges which actually remove the material being drilled; spiral flutes running up the shank of the drill clear waste from the hole as the drill works. They come in sizes up to about 13mm (½in). For larger holes you can use either a wood bit and a carpenter's brace or a flat wood bit fitted into a power drill.

What to do

Start by selecting a twist drill or wood bit to match the diameter of the hole you want to drill, and fit it into the jaws (known as the chuck) of your hand drill, brace or power drill. Make sure the chuck grips the drill or bit securely.

In almost every case you will be drilling a hole at right angles to the wood surface, so it is important to line the tool up carefully before you start drilling. This gets easier with a little experience, but to begin with you can sight the drill against a try square set on end alongside it.

With a hand drill, simply turn the cranked handle while maintaining steady downward pressure with your other hand.

With a brace, guide the tool with one hand on the dome-shaped head while you turn the crank with the other. Most have a ratchet mechanism that allows the tool to be used in tight corners where a full 360° sweep of the handle is not possible.

With a power drill, simply align the drill bit and squeeze the trigger.

What you need:
- hand drill *or*
- carpenter's brace *or*
- power drill
- twist drills or wood bits
- cramps or portable workbench
- try square as drilling guide

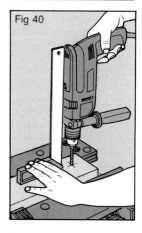

Fig 40

Fig 40 Stand your try square next to the drill to help you keep the drill body vertical.

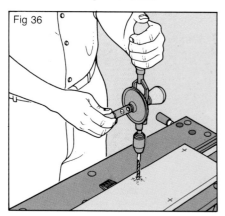

Fig 36

Fig 37

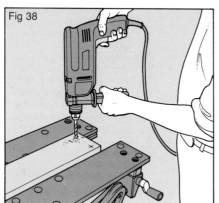

Fig 38

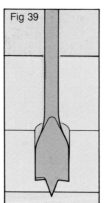

Fig 39

Fig 36 Use a hand drill and a twist drill bit to make small holes by hand. Keep the drill vertical as you work.

Fig 37 Use a brace and wood bit for making large-diameter holes. The ratchet operation of the crank allows you to work in confined spaces.

Fig 38 Hold a power drill in both hands as you drill holes, keeping your eye over the drilling line.

Fig 39 When using wood bits in power drills, work from one side first until the lead point breaks through. Then complete the hole from the other side to avoid splintering.

Smoothing and Shaping Wood

Once you have cut the wood you are working on to the size you want, your next task is to smooth off the cut end; sawing will have left it rather ragged, especially with natural timber and boards such as plywood made with natural timber veneers. The simplest way of doing this is to use an abrasive material such as sandpaper (more properly known as glasspaper; sand is no longer used as the abrasive grit). This is available in a wide range of grades from coarse to fine; stick with the finer grades unless your sawing was a little inaccurate and you need to remove larger amounts of wood to get back to your original marked cutting line.

You can use hand sanding to smooth the planed surfaces of off-the-shelf timber and man-made boards too, ready for it to be given a decorative finish such as paint or varnish. Here you should always sand parallel with the grain direction, to avoid scoring the wood surface.

You can take the hard work out of sanding large areas of wood or boards by using a power sander.

What to do

If you are hand-sanding, you need to take care not to round off the edges of the workpiece as you sand it (unless, of course, this is the effect you want.) The best way of avoiding this is to cut the abrasive sheet down into narrow strips and to fold one round a sanding block. This ensures that the abrasive sheet remains flat against the cut end of your workpiece.

If you prefer to use a power sander for finishing work, the best tool to use is the orbital sander. This takes cut-to-size sheets of abrasive paper in various grades, and is ideal for finishing larger areas such as doors ready for decorating. Fitted with coarse abrasive, it can also remove larger amounts of wood.

To begin with at least, you are likely to be working mainly with off-the-shelf planed timber. However, there may be times when you need to reduce the size of something by more than an orbital sander can reasonably cope with. There are a range of planer-files ideal for this task.

What you need:
- abrasive paper plus sanding block *or*
- power sander plus sanding sheets
- Surform file or block plane

CHECK
- that you keep the sanding block or sander baseplate square to the workpiece when sanding end grain, to avoid rounding off edges and corners.
- that you use the correct grade of abrasive paper – coarse for removing a lot of wood, medium for general sanding and fine for finishing work.
- that you always sand along the grain direction.

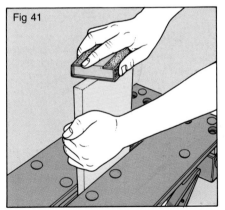

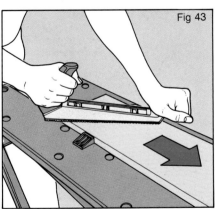

Fig 41 Sand cut ends of timber and board with abrasive paper wrapped round a sanding block.

Fig 42 Alternatively, use an orbital sander to smooth the cut end. Keep the sanding pad flat on the workpiece.

Fig 43 To remove larger amounts of wood, use a rasp held at an angle to the wood grain and moved parallel to it along the workpiece.

Fig 44 Use a Surform block plane for smaller shaping jobs such as easing the edges of sticking doors.

23

Using Nails and Adhesives

The simplest way of joining two pieces of wood together is to use nails. These come in a wide range of types and sizes (*see* page 91 for more details), and are simply driven into the wood using a hammer. Nailing is ideal for simple butt joints (the corners of a box, for example) where the joint will not be under any stress; the one drawback with nails is that they will pull out under load. Nailing is also widely used for pinning thin cladding materials such as hardboard or plywood to solid timber frames.

Where you want to give a simple butt joint of this type some extra strength, the solution is to use woodworking adhesive along the bond line – either on its own, or more commonly in conjunction with nailing. Modern woodworking adhesives are easy to use straight from the bottle – a far cry from grandpa's bubbling hot glue pot – and give a very strong bond. Water-resistant types can also be used out of doors.

The one thing to remember about using glued joints is that they are very difficult to dismantle.

What to do

Start by selecting the correct type of nail for the fixing you want to make. The oval wire nail is the most widely used for general woodwork. Before driving it into the wood, align its shank so the longer cross-section is parallel with the direction of the wood grain; this reduces the risk of the nail splitting the wood if it is driven in near the end of the workpiece. Hold the nail between finger and thumb and tap it with the hammer so it stands up on its own. Then drive it fully home, using a nail punch to recess its head slightly so you do not dent the workpiece with the hammer head.

Use the wedge-shaped end (called the pein) of a pin hammer to start small pins, then reverse the hammer head to complete the operation.

For glued joints, spread adhesive along one of the surfaces to be joined and then press them firmly together – ideally with cramps to hold the joint securely until the adhesive has set.

What you need:
- claw or pin hammer
- nails or pins (*see* page 91 for more details)
- nail punch
- woodworking adhesive

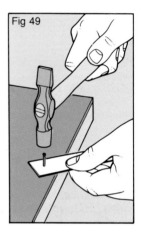

Fig 49 Push pins and tacks too small to hold through a piece of paper, and use this to hold the pin in place while you start it.

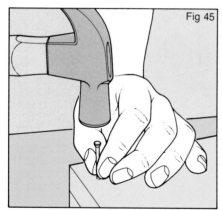

Fig 45

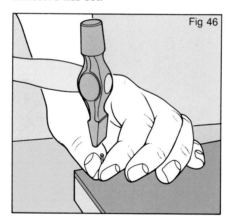

Fig 46

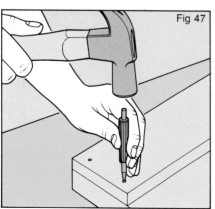

Fig 47

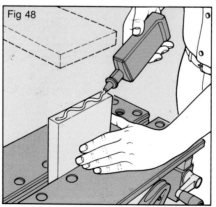

Fig 48

Fig 45 To start a nail, hold it between your finger and thumb and tap its head gently. Then drive it with firm hammer blows.

Fig 46 Start small pins with the wedge end of a cross-pein hammer.

Fig 47 Use a pin punch to drive nail heads just below the wood surface; this avoids any risk of marking the wood with the hammer head.

Fig 48 Reinforce nailed joints with woodworking adhesive, and support the joint while the adhesive sets.

Using Screws

Screws provide a method of joining wood to wood that is far superior to either nails or adhesives. The design of the threaded shank draws the two components being joined tightly together as the screw is driven in, and the fixing is strongly resistant to being pulled apart by stress on the joint. Yet the screw can be withdrawn just as easily if the joint has to be dismantled. The fixing can be concealed by recessing the screw head into the wood, or it can be left to show.

The one drawback with using screws is that, unlike nails, they cannot simply be driven straight into the wood. The size and shape of the shank will split the wood unless a clearance hole is drilled through one component to accept the shank, and a pilot hole is drilled in the other component to accept the threaded section. In addition, if the screw head is to be hidden, a conical recess called a countersink must also be formed. This is time-consuming, and must also be carried out with precision if the resulting joint is to be assembled square and properly aligned.

What to do

Start by choosing a screw at least twice as long as the thickness of the wood you are fixing. For most woodworking projects you will be using countersunk screws; for extra grip use special screws with fully-threaded shanks for fixings into man-made boards such as chipboard and fibreboard.

Position the two pieces of wood you are joining over each other, and clamp them to your bench. Drill a pilot hole through both pieces at the fixing position, using a depth stop so that the depth of the hole is just less than the screw length. Now drill the larger clearance hole through just the upper piece of wood using the pilot hole as a guide. Finally, form the countersink with a countersinking bit. (see page 90 for details of the correct hole sizes to drill for each gauge of screw).

As you drive the screw in, use the non-driving hand to steady the screwdriver blade in the slot so it cannot slip out and damage the surface of the workpiece. Do not over-tighten it or you may break it.

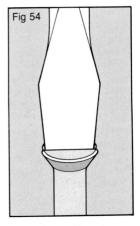

Fig 54 Screwdriver tips must fit slotted screw heads precisely.

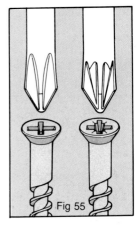

Fig 55 Cross-point screwdrivers with Phillips point (*left*) and Pozidriv point (*right*).

Fig 50 Screwed joints need countersunk and clearance holes in one component and a pilot hole in the other.

Fig 51 Chipboard screws are threaded right up to the screw head for improved grip.

Fig 52 Use a depth stop to gauge the correct depth of pilot holes.

Fig 53 Use a counter-sinking bit to drill the cone-shaped recess for the screw head.

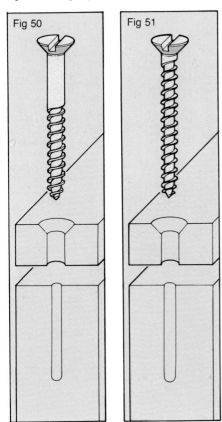

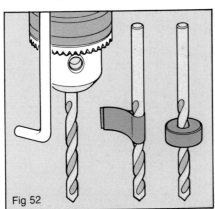

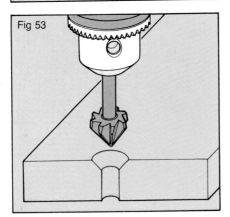

Using Joint Blocks

Nails make relatively weak fixings unless the joint is also glued, while screws take time to place accurately and do not make very strong fixings in fibrous man-made boards such as chipboard. Since this is one of the most popular materials for much do-it-yourself furniture, especially in the form of off-the-shelf planks with a veneer or plastic surface, there is clearly a need for some means of forming simple corner joints that are both relatively strong and also easy for the amateur to assemble. Joint blocks are the answer.

The simplest types comprise a single block which is fixed into the angle between the two pieces being joined. Some are screwed first to one component, then to the other; another type is screwed to one piece and is then push-fitted into a hole drilled in the other. More complex types have two mating parts; one is attached to each component, then the two are locked together by either a machine screw (a small bolt) or by rotating a locking cam within the body of the block. Their one drawback is that they remain visible.

What to do

Start by cutting the components to be joined to length, and check that the cut ends are square. Then place the two pieces together so you can mark the position of the joint block in the angle between them. Use two blocks on components up to about 230mm (9in) wide, three for wider boards.

With one-piece blocks, simply screw the block to one component at its marked position, then offer up the second component and drive the fixing screw through the block or locate the flanged lug in a hole drilled in the second component to complete the joint.

With two-part blocks, separate the parts and fix one to the first component of the joint, the other to the second. Check the alignment carefully, then lock the two parts together with the screw or cam. Note that with standard two-part blocks, each part is inset from the edge of the board, while with cam-type fixings the part containing the rotating cam is fitted flush with the board edge.

What you need:
- joint blocks
- wood screws
- drill plus twist drill bits (some types only)
- screwdriver

TIP
Always mark up the block positions carefully, then fix one component of the joint and check the fit before completing the assembly.

CHECK
- that bolts or machine screws securing two-part blocks are tight.
- that cam fixings are fully engaged and tightened.

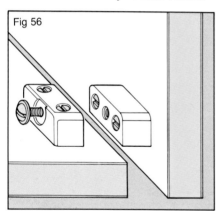

Fig 56

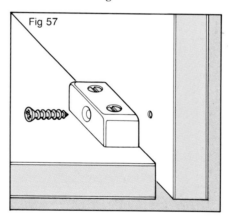

Fig 57

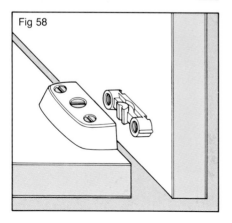

Fig 58

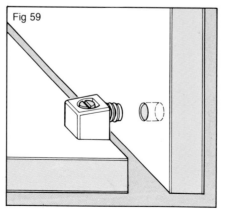

Fig 59

Fig 56 The standard two-part joint block. Screw one part to each component being joined, and then fix the blocks together with the machine screw.

Fig 57 Screw one-part blocks to one component, then drive a screw through the block into the other component.

Fig 58 With locking cam fittings, position the blocks carefully and then push them together, turning the integral screw to rotate the cam and lock the two blocks together.

Fig 59 With lightweight fixings, glue the projecting peg of the block into the hole in the second component.

Making Dowel Joints

If you are working with man-made boards and want a corner or T-joint that is both strong (unlike nails or screws) and invisible (unlike joint blocks, which can also be relatively expensive to use in large numbers), one of the neatest and strongest joints you can use is the dowel joint. The dowels themselves are short hardwood pegs which are glued into holes drilled in the two components, forming a joint that is rigid and easy to assemble especially if you use a dowelling jig to ensure that the holes are drilled in the right positions and to the right depth.

You can drill the holes with ordinary twist drills, but you will get better results with a special dowelling bit, which has a centre point to make it easy to position the bit precisely and which drills flat-bottomed holes. Buy one with an adjustable depth stop mounted on its shank. If you are not using a jig you will also need some special metal dowel pins which are used to mark the dowel positions on the second component once you have drilled the holes in the first one.

What to do

If you are working free-hand, start by marking up the components you are joining together so you can decide where to position the dowels. For a corner joint, for example, mark the edge thickness of one component on the face of the other and then mark the dowel positions along the centre line of the joint. Drill holes for the dowels to just over half the thickness of the component using the depth stop, and check that the dowels you are using are a good fit – tight but removable. Then insert a dowel pin in each hole and butt up the second component so the pins mark the mating hole positions on its end. Drill the holes, glue and insert the dowels into one component and then add more glue to the projecting dowel ends before assembling the joint. Wipe off any excess adhesive that is forced out of the joint.

With a dowelling jig, simply assemble the components in the jig as directed by the manufacturer's instructions and then drill the holes, ready for the dowels.

What you need:
- pre-cut fluted dowels
- dowelling bit
- hand *or* power drill
- depth stop
- pencil *or* marking knife
- dowel pins *or* dowelling jig

CHECK
- that you mark the dowel positions accurately so they are centred on the end of one component of the joint.
- that you do not drill too deep into the other component.

TIP
Apply woodworking adhesive to each end of the dowel in turn as you assemble the joint, and wipe away any excess that oozes out. Do not squirt adhesive into the dowel holes.

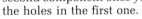

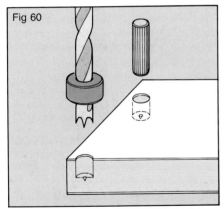

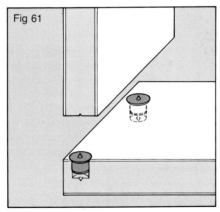

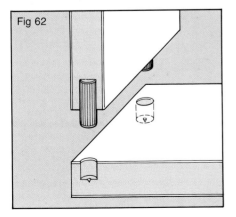

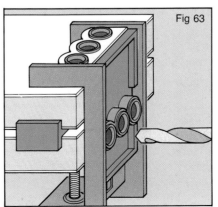

Fig 60 Use a dowelling bit and depth stop to drill holes for the dowels to about half the thickness of the first component.

Fig 61 Insert dowel pins into the holes and offer up the second component to mark the position of its dowel holes. Remove the pins and drill the holes.

Fig 62 Insert the glued dowels in the holes in one component, then offer this up to the second component to complete the joint. Cramp it up square while the adhesive sets.

Fig 63 Use a dowelling jig to ensure that dowel holes are correctly placed and accurately drilled.

Making 'Proper' Joints

The joints described so far, made using nails, screws, joint blocks or dowels, are all simple butt or overlap joints relying for their strength on whatever is fixing the two joint components together. However, you may well want to make joints that look neater and more attractive than butt joints, especially if you are making framed furniture and similar items from natural timber. Learning to make the group of joints covered here will widen your woodworking repertoire considerably, as well as increasing your woodworking skills.

Two of them, the **mitre** joint and the **edge** joint, are, in a sense, still butt joints. The former is mainly used to hide the exposed end-grain of the wood and to give an attractively symmetrical look to things like picture frames and mouldings round door and window openings. The latter is used to create wide boards from narrower pieces of natural timber – to make a table top, for example.

The other four joints featured here not only look pleasing to the eye; they also interlock to give the joint extra strength.

What to do

Mitre joints A basic mitre joint consists of two pieces of wood with their ends cut at 45° and assembled to form a right-angled joint. This is usually glued and pinned, but can be reinforced with dowels set in the mating surfaces at right angles to the mitre cuts. You can mark up the 45° angles with a combination square, but it is easier to use a bench aid called a mitre box which guides the saw blade at precisely the right angle. With the two mitres cut, fit the joint together dry and use your try square to check that the joint is a true right angle before assembling it.

Halving joints A halving joint is what its name implies – a joint formed by removing half of each component so that the two interlock when the joint is assembled. It can be used at corners, in which case all you need to cut each half is a tenon saw, or as a T-joint, which needs a chisel too. For accurate marking-up of the joint you need your marking gauge, set to precisely half the thickness of the wood being joined.

What you need:
- tape measure
- try square
- combination square *or* protractor for mitre joints
- marking gauge for halving joints
- mortise gauge for mortise-and-tenon joints
- pencil *or* marking knife
- tenon saw
- chisel and mallet
- power drill, wood bit and depth stop

CHECK
- that joints fit accurately together when dry before gluing them up.
- that joints are square when assembled.
- that joints are cramped while the adhesive sets.

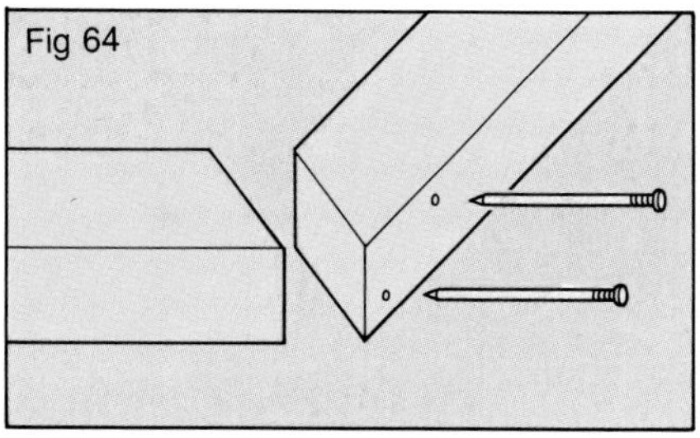

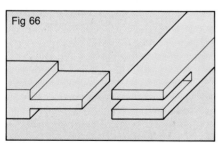

Fig 64

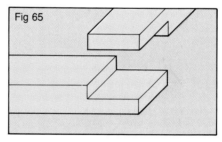

Fig 65

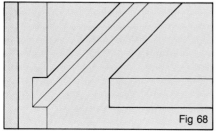

Fig 66

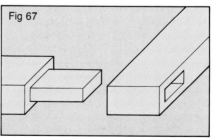

Fig 67

Fig 68

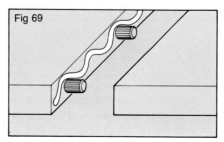

Fig 69

Fig 64 The mitred joint needs gluing and pinning to make a secure joint.

Fig 65 The corner halving joint can be cut with a tenon saw. It should be glued and can be strengthened with pins or screws.

Fig 66 The bridle joint offers increased gluing area and greater bond strength. You need a chisel to cut the slot.

Fig 67 The mortise-and-tenon joint is ideal for joining rails in framed constructions. It is always glued, and may be screwed or pegged with dowels too. You need a chisel to cut the mortise.

Fig 68 The housing joint is mainly used to support things like shelf ends. You need a long chisel or a router to cut the groove.

Fig 69 Edge-to-edge joints are simple butt joints, always glued and usually also reinforced with dowels.

Making 'Proper' Joints

Bridle joints These are similar to halving joints in principle, but are stronger because of the increased area of contact between the two components. A slot equal to one-third of the wood's thickness is cut in the end of one component, and the outer third is cut away from each face of the other component to allow the slot to fit over it, as shown here. Bridle joints can also be used as T-joints.

Mortise-and-tenon joints These consist of a projecting peg (the tenon) cut on the end of one component which fits in a matching hole (the mortise) cut in the other. For corner joints the tenon is reduced in width, as shown here, and it may be cut shorter and fitted into a stopped mortise (one that does not pass right through the wood) to form a joint with no end grain visible once it is assembled. You need a mortise gauge to mark the joint out, plus a tenon saw and chisel to cut it. You can make cutting the mortise easier if you drill out most of the waste first with a wood bit, using the chisel to square up the hole ready to receive the tenon.

Housing joints These are mainly used to form a strong joint where the horizontal board will be carrying a heavy load, as in a bookcase. You need a tenon saw and chisel (or a power router) to cut the housing, which is usually half the thickness of the board into which it is set.

Edge joints These are usually assembled as glued butt joints; accurate dowel positioning is essential for a perfect joint.

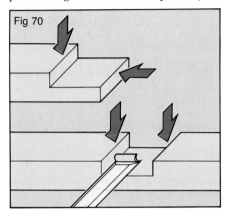

Fig 70

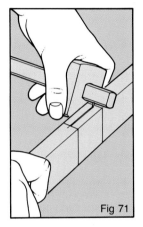

Fig 71

Fig 70 Make tenon saw cuts first, then remove waste with a chisel.

Fig 71 Mark the joint with a marking gauge.

Fig 72 Mark mitres with a combination square.

Fig 73 Cut mitres using a mitre block.

Fig 74 Drill mortises. . .

Fig 75 . . . then square them up with a chisel.

Fig 76 Trim tenons with a chisel for a good fit.

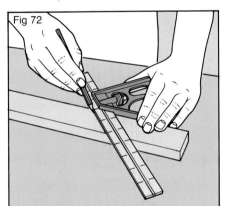

Fig 72

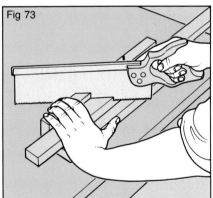

Fig 73

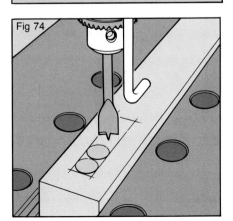

Fig 74

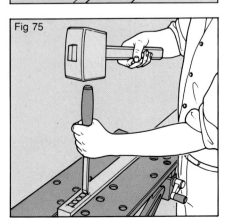

Fig 75

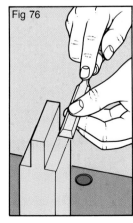

Fig 76

Scribing and Cramping

Scribing is an operation you will often have to carry out in order to make things fit around the house, especially as far as installing built-in furniture is concerned. Unfortunately wall and ceiling surfaces, especially in older homes, are rarely true and so to avoid unsightly gaps you need to be able to transcribe onto your workpiece the contours of the surface against which it will be fitted – the rear edge of a shelf in an alcove, for example.

What to do

The technique of scribing involves placing your workpiece next to the surface against which it will fit and then using an offcut of wood and a pencil to copy the surface profile onto the workpiece. Tape the pencil to the block so it is a little further from the end of the block than the biggest gap between surface and workpiece. Then press the block against the surface being copied and run it along the workpiece. The pencil will draw out the surface profile ready for cutting – the perfect job for a jig saw.

Cramping is used to hold workpieces together for all sorts of woodworking operations, from marking out joints to holding components together while adhesive sets. You can often improvise cramps, but you will get better results by including at least a pair of traditional G-cramps or modern quick-release cramps in your tool-kit. You will also find the jaws of a portable workbench useful for big jobs.

What to do

Use G-cramps or quick-release cramps to hold components securely together while marking up or drilling joints, and also for securing workpieces to the bench for operations such as cutting mortises. Always use scrap wood as packing to prevent the jaws from marking the workpiece. You can also use them to hold guide battens when making long cuts with a jigsaw.

Use the wide-capacity jaws of a portable workbench to hold boards together when making edge joints, and also to hold completed assemblies such as boxes.

What you need:
For scribing:
- pencil
- wood offcut
- adhesive tape

For cramping:
- cramps or portable workbench
- scrap wood for packing

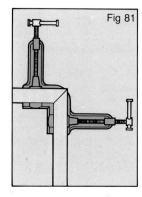

Fig 81 Special mitre cramps are invaluable for holding mitre joint components together.

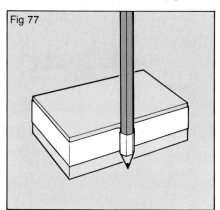

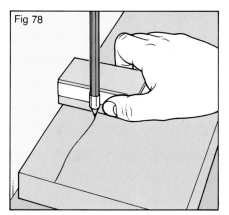

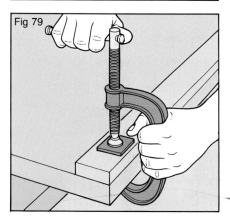

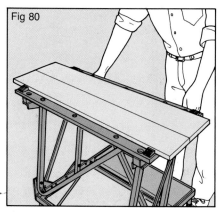

Fig 77 Make a scribing block by taping a pencil to a small offcut.

Fig 78 To scribe a wall profile onto the rear edge of a shelf, hold the board against the wall and run the block along it so it presses against the wall. Then cut along the scribed line with a jigsaw.

Fig 79 Use cramps to hold glued components together until the adhesive has set. Fit small packing pieces of scrap wood between the jaws and the workpiece to prevent marks as you tighten the cramp jaws.

Fig 80 Use a portable workbench as a giant vice for cramping up edge joints and other large components.

INDOOR JOBS

As far as working with wood is concerned, there are a great many home improvement projects you can carry out inside the house. They range from the simple tasks such as putting up shelves that just about every householder carries out at some time or another, to more complex projects such as hanging new doors or dividing large rooms with timber stud partition walls. All of the jobs covered in this chapter are well within the capabilities of any amateur woodworker, and since many of them are fairly labour-intensive, carrying them out yourself will save a great deal of money compared with the cost of calling in a professional to do the work for you.

Whatever you decide to tackle, you will find the necessary materials and fittings widely available from all the regular do-it-yourself suppliers. All you need are the basic skills to do the work and the time and will to complete the job.

What you can tackle

You do not have to be a master joiner and cabinet-maker to carry out many of the most popular home improvement projects in wood. Here are some examples.

Shelving There is an enormous variety of shelving systems on the market nowadays, enabling you to put up anything from a single small shelf to a run of wall-to-wall storage. Even the shelves come pre-packed and ready to install. For most systems all you need to do is to make a series of secure wall fixings to support whatever type of bracket or track you have chosen.

Kit furniture You can easily install a new fitted kitchen or a run of wardrobes using flat-packed kit furniture. The basic raw material of these kits is veneered or plastic-coated chipboard, with all the panels not only cut to size but often complete with all the necessary fittings, hinges, catches and so on. All you need to put them together are some simple tools.

New doors The choice of different door styles available has never been larger, and replacing either your external doors or internal doors can effect a dramatic transformation in your home's appearance. All you have to master is the art of fitting hinges and door furniture.

Home security Improving home security is high on the list of every householder's priorities nowadays. There is a wide range of easy-to-fit locks and other security devices available for doors and windows, and the cost of installing them is more than outweighed by the extra peace of mind that having them brings.

Decorative trims Every home contains a range of decorative timber mouldings – door and window architraves, skirting boards, perhaps picture and dado rails, all of which may be looking rather down at heel. Replacing them could be part of a major refurbishment scheme, as could fitting timber cladding to walls or ceilings.

Stair handrails One of the most popular home improvements of recent years has been the fitting of new handrails and balusters on stairs and landings, thanks to the availability of a range of attractive mouldings and other stair parts. These enable you to restore time-ravaged balustrades to something approaching their original glory with comparative ease.

Room partitions One comparatively major task you could undertake is the building of internal partition walls to make better use of your existing floor space. The carpentry involved is relatively straightforward, even if you have to get professional help with the plastering.

Fig 82 (*above*) Indoors, your woodworking skills can be put to many uses, from making furniture to stripping wood floors, replacing skirting boards and architraves, even framing pictures.

Putting up Shelves

Shelves are a basic requirement in almost every room in the house. They are needed for displaying ornaments and books or housing home entertainment equipment in the living room, for providing storage space in the kitchen, for stacking kids' toys and games in their bedrooms, and many other jobs. Whatever their use, the first thing you have to decide is where you want them, how many you will need, and how long and wide each shelf will need to be. Think too about materials, not only in terms of looks but also of performance; remember that man-made boards – especially chipboard – are not good at carrying heavy loads unless they are very well supported (see TIP).

Choosing the Supports

You can support shelves on the wall in a variety of ways. One of the most popular locations for shelving is in alcoves, and here you can fix supports to the alcove walls for the shelf ends (and for the rear edge too, if necessary.) You can use timber battens or L-shaped metal angle strip for fixed shelves, while proprietary book-case strip or shelf support pegs fixed to the alcove sides can provide an easily adjustable shelving system.

For 'free-standing' shelves, the obvious choices are either to use one of the many track support systems, or to use individual shelf brackets of one type or another.

What you need:
- shelves
- shelf support battens, brackets or track
- woodscrews and wallplugs
- tape measure
- try square
- pencil or marking knife
- hand or power saw
- spirit level
- bradawl
- power drill plus twist and masonry drills
- screwdriver

TIP
Do not exceed the manufacturer's recommended bracket spacings or your shelves will sag under heavy loads.

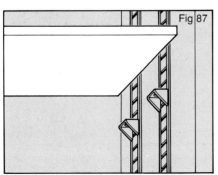

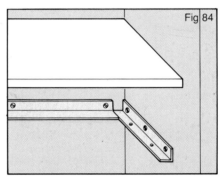

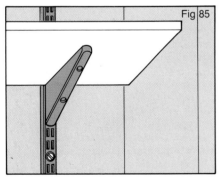

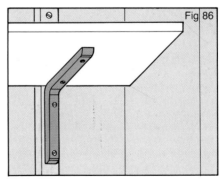

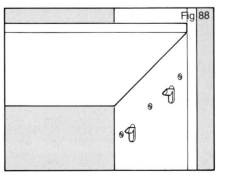

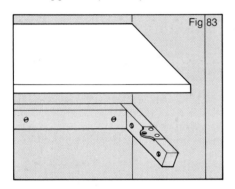

Fig 83 One of the least inexpensive ways of fitting shelves in alcoves is to support them on battens screwed to the walls. Use small mirror plates to secure the shelves to the battens.

Fig 84 An alternative to battens is to use L-section aluminium channelling.

Fig 85 Adjustable track shelving systems need no end supports, but take care to fit the tracks level and parallel.

Fig 86 Individual shelf brackets are easier to position accurately if you screw them to slim wall battens first.

Fig 87 Bookcase strip provides unobtrusive shelf-end support, and the shelves are fully adjustable.

Fig 88 One of the cheapest methods is to use shelf support studs set in holes drilled in side panels fitted within the alcove.

Putting up Shelves

What to do: Alcove Shelving

If you want to fit shelves in alcoves, one of the simplest and most economical methods is to screw slim timber battens to the side walls of the recess to support the shelf ends. Start by deciding on the precise shelf position (and the shelf spacing if you want several shelves), and mark one side wall. Use a spirit level to draw a truly horizontal line to indicate the shelf position, and fix the batten to the wall immediately below the line.

Next, measure the alcove width and cut the shelf to length. Rest one end on the fixed batten, lay your spirit level on the shelf and raise or lower the position of the second batten until the shelf is absolutely level. Mark and fix the second batten, and lay the shelf in place.

If the alcove is out of square, use a pair of slim battens held together with rubber bands to measure the alcove width at several points. Transfer these to the shelf so you can cut its ends to match the irregular alcove width.

Fig 89 (*above*) Putting up shelves is one of the simplest and most rewarding of DIY woodworking jobs.

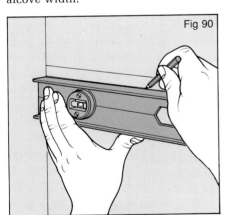

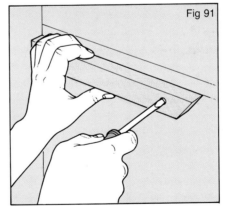

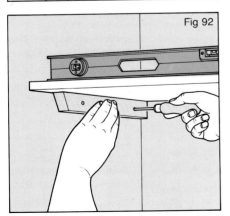

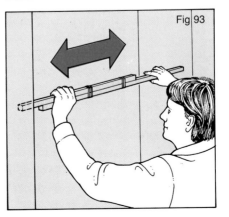

Fig 90 Decide on the shelf positions and mark true horizontal lines on one side wall.

Fig 91 Drill clearance holes in the battens, mark the screw positions, drill and plug the holes and fit the batten.

Fig 92 Lay the shelf on the fixed batten, hold the second batten under its other end and check that the shelf is level. Mark the positions of the screw holes, fix the batten and add the shelf.

Fig 93 In out-of-square alcoves, use two battens held together with rubber bands to gauge the alcove width.

Putting up Shelves

What to do: Track Shelving

Track shelving is one of the most popular adjustable shelf support systems for free-standing shelves, and can be used in alcoves too. The tracks which carry the brackets are simply screwed to the wall at the appropriate spacing, although care must be taken to fix them level and parallel.

Start by marking the track positions on the wall. Then drill and plug a hole for the top fixing screw of the first track, and drive the screw partly home. Use a spirit level to check that the track is vertical, and mark the other screw positions. Swing the track aside while you drill and plug them, then drive all the fixing screws fully home.

Next, use a batten and your spirit level to mark the position of the top of the other track, and repeat the same sequence of operations to fix it to the wall. Fit the brackets at the desired spacings and lay the shelves in place. Unless they are in an alcove, it is a good idea to screw each shelf to its bracket for stability.

Fig 94 (*above*) Track shelving is the easiest way of providing fully adjustable shelving.

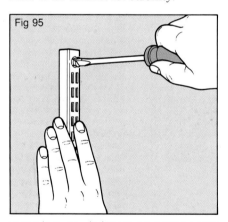

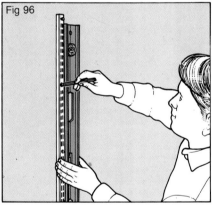

Fig 95 Decide on the best positions for the track and hang the first length with just its top screw.

Fig 96 Use a spirit level to check that the track is vertical and mark the other screw positions on the wall.

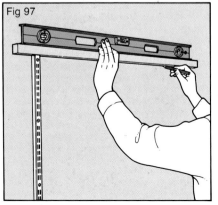

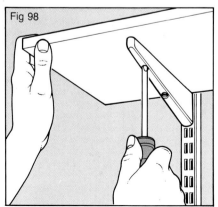

Fig 97 Fix the other screws, then use a batten and spirit level to mark where the top of the other track will be sited.

Fig 98 Fit the second track, then slot in the brackets and attach the shelves to them to stop them sliding or being knocked sideways.

Putting up Shelves

What to do: Individual Brackets

For a short, narrow shelf on individual brackets, it is easiest to fix the brackets to the underside of the shelf first. Then hold the shelf against the wall with a spirit level on top, mark the positions of the bracket fixing screws, drill and plug the wall and drive the screws.

For longer, wider shelves, start by marking the bracket positions on the underside of the shelf, and use an end one to mark the position of an end bracket on the wall. Fix this bracket to the wall. Then rest the shelf on it with a spirit level on top so you can mark the position at the other end bracket. Fix this in place too, then rest the shelf on top and mark the wall so you can fit the remaining brackets. Finally, screw the brackets to the shelves.

Fig 105 To fit several shelves one above the other using individual brackets, mark up wall battens and fix the brackets to these first. Then secure the battens to the wall as for track shelving.

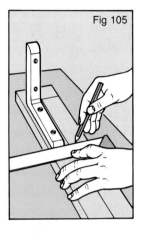

Fig 105

Fig 99

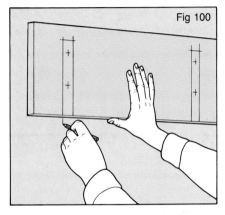

Fig 100

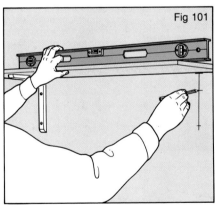

Fig 101

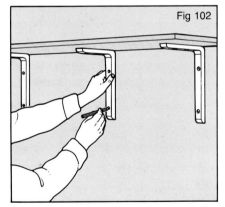

Fig 102

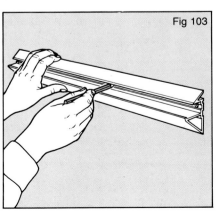

Fig 103

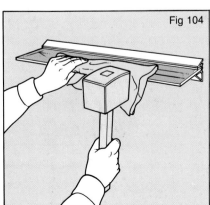

Fig 104

Fig 99 To put up a short shelf with individual brackets, screw the brackets on first. Then hold the shelf against the wall and mark the positions of the fixing screws.

Fig 100 With longer shelves, mark the bracket positions on the shelf and transfer the first bracket position to the wall.

Fig 101 Hold the shelf level while you mark the second bracket position.

Fig 102 Screw the brackets to the shelf, then to the wall.

Fig 103 With one-piece shelf edge supports, draw a horizontal line on the wall and mark the screw positions.

Fig 104 Screw the support to the wall, then tap in the shelf.

Fitting Floor-Standing Furniture

The most popular – and widely available – types of free-standing furniture for home assembly are kitchen and bedroom units. These come in carry-home packs containing all the necessary panels, doors, drawers and fittings, and all you have to do is to follow the manufacturer's instructions to put them together. You can also buy simple items of free-standing furniture such as side tables, stools and chests of drawers in flat-pack form.

Assembling these kits takes little more than some ingenuity (many of the instruction leaflets are not exactly models of clarity) and a few simple tools. Modern knock-down fittings make sturdy joints that are generally quick to assemble, and hinges and drawer runners are easy to add ready for the doors and drawers (the latter also in kit form) to be fitted.

The biggest problem lies in installing a run of these box-type units in a room so that they stand squarely and line up neatly with each other; floors are rarely perfectly level and walls are seldom square to each other, even in modern homes.

What to do

If you are installing a run of kitchen or bedroom units, it is wise to spend some time surveying the room in which they will be fitted. The first step is to establish whether the floor has any high spots, so you can take these as the base level.

For example, if you are fitting a run of kitchen base units, take one cabinet side panel and stand it at right angles against the room wall at various points along each wall where the units will stand. Mark where its top edge meets the wall at each point, then draw a horizontal line on the wall round the room with a batten and spirit level, working from one of the marks. If any of your intermediate marks lie above this line, redraw the horizontal line so it passes through the highest mark. This will then mark the position of the bottom edge of the worktop, and will enable you to see which units need some packing beneath them (or adjustments to their feet) to keep them level with neighbouring units standing on the floor's high spots.

What you need:
Flat-pack furniture
- furniture kit
- screwdrivers to fit screws or bolts in assembly fittings
- clear instructions
- patience!

DIY furniture:
- timber and board
- measuring, marking, cutting, drilling and assembling tools as required
- assembly fittings as required.

CHECK
- that all the parts and fittings are present in flat-pack furniture kits as soon as you get the units home, and that panels are undamaged.

TIP
Assemble carcases on a flat, level surface so you can check that they are square. Leave fitting drawers and doors until the units are set in position.

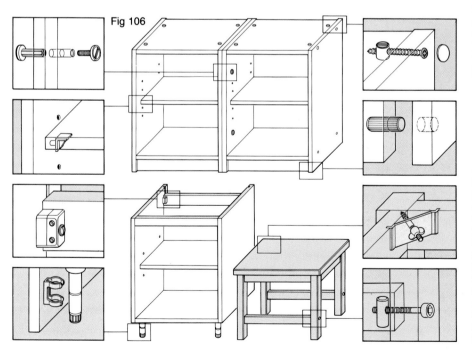

Fig 106

Fig 106 Floor-standing furniture – especially the flat-pack variety – is assembled in a number of ways. Corners may be fixed with joint blocks, cam fittings, screw plates or screws locking into hidden dowels. Shelves are generally supported on shelf pegs, while plinths may be clipped to adjustable feet. Connector screws hold runs of units together.

Fitting Floor-Standing Furniture

If the run includes tall units with upper doors that need to align with the doors on wall-hung units, stand a side panel from each one in position and mark the level of its upper door on the wall. Extend this line round the room too, to indicate the position of the wall units. Otherwise simply measure up from your worktop level and mark a line for the wall units at a comfortable height for whoever will be using them. As a general guide you need about 400mm (16in) clearance between the worktop and the underside of the wall units to avoid banging your head on them.

Now assemble the individual units, minus doors and drawers to make them easier to handle during installation, but adding internal fittings such as drawer runners while they are easy to get at. Start by fitting a corner unit so you can establish the correct fitting level along two adjacent walls. Add packing beneath the unit, or adjust its screw feet if these are fitted, to get the unit level with the wall line. Check that it is standing level from front to back too, then secure it to the wall.

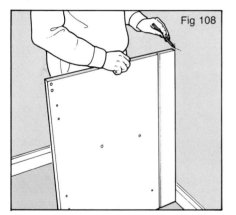

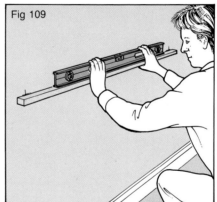

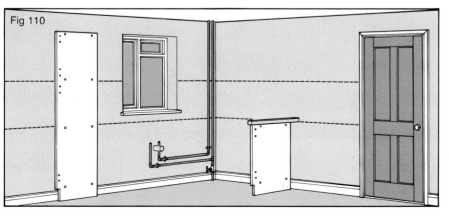

Fig 107 (*above*) Fitting your own kitchen units is not difficult if you know the tricks of the trade.

Fig 108 Floors are never level, so start by using a side panel to find the high spots. Make marks at intervals all round the room.

Fig 109 Draw a horizontal line through one of the marks, and check which other mark is the furthest above it.

Fig 110 Redraw the line through the highest mark, along all walls against which units will stand. Use a side panel from a tall unit to mark the line of the wall cupboards too.

Fitting Floor-Standing Furniture

Where there are pipes or other obstructions on the back wall, mark the positions of cut-outs to match them on the unit's side panels and saw them out carefully with a jig saw or coping saw. Push the unit back into place so you can check its fit round the obstruction.

As you align neighbouring units, fix them together with connector bolts to enhance the rigidity of the run. Carry on working round the room, adding units one by one until the installation is complete. Then you can fit the doors, adjusting the hinges so they sit level with each other and open and close smoothly, and make up drawer kits ready for installing on their runners. Finally, add the plinth sections by screwing them to the front edges of the units' side panels or by clipping them to the screw feet if these are fitted.

What you need:
For fitting units:
- pencil
- tape measure
- straight-edge
- spirit level
- screwdrivers
- scrap wood or hardboard for packing
- power drill plus twist and masonry bits
- screws and wallplugs

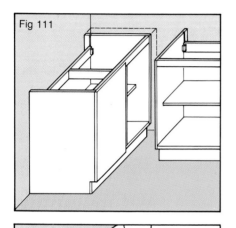

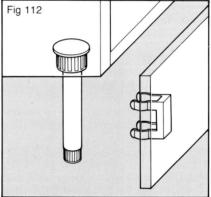

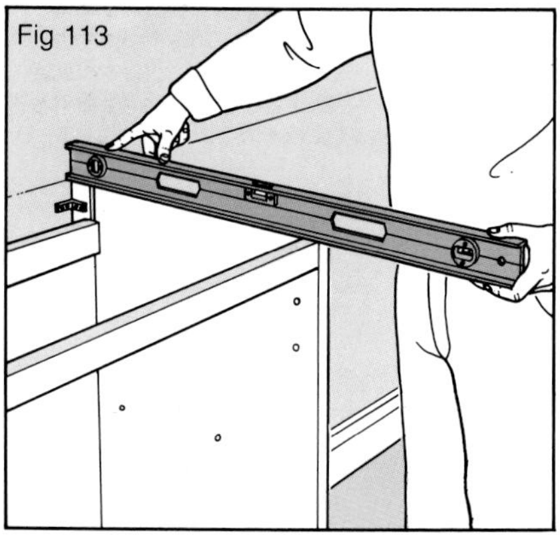

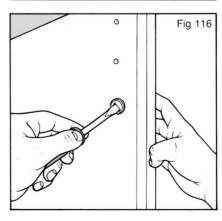

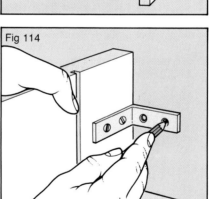

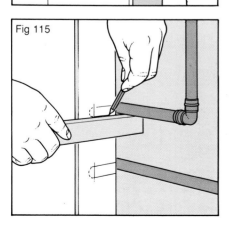

Fig 111 Start positioning floor-standing units in a corner, to ensure that the run is correctly levelled along two adjacent walls.

Fig 112 Many units now have adjustable feet to make levelling easy. Otherwise, insert packing slips beneath the unit sides to bring them level with the line marked on the wall.

Fig 113 Check that units are level from front to back as well as from side to side.

Fig 114 When each unit is standing level and square, fix it to the wall using angle brackets, joint blocks or by driving screws through back rails as appropriate.

Fig 115 Mark and remove small cut-outs where necessary to allow the units' side panels to fit round obstructions such as pipework.

Fig 116 Finally, use connector screws to link adjacent units together and form a rigid and stable assembly.

Fitting Wall-Hung Units

Kitchen wall units. and other wall-hung cupboards and shelving units sold in flat-pack form, are generally fixed to the wall with proprietary hanging brackets. Start by making up the unit carcases, minus their doors, as directed by the instructions.

What to do

If the unit has an internal bracket which you screw directly to the wall, offer it up to its fixing line (with a helper for heavy units) so you can mark the screw positions on the wall. Drill and plug the holes and screw the cabinet to the wall.

Many units now have one- or two-part brackets, which are often adjustable. The former are screwed to the rear of the unit and locate on a screw driven into the wall. The latter have one part screwed to the cabinet, the other to the wall, and the two parts interlock to provide a firm fixing. On timber-framed walls, make sure fixings are made directly into the studs or else to a solid batten fixed between them. Never rely on cavity fittings.

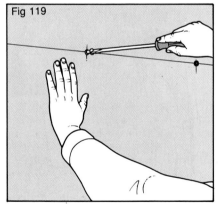

Fig 117 (*above*) Position wall units at a height that avoids bumped heads but allows the contents to be reached easily.

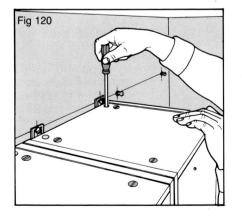

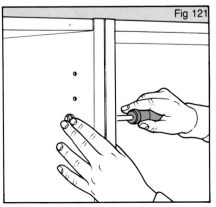

Fig 118 Check the type of fixings supplied with your wall units, and mark the fixing positions on the wall.

Fig 119 Drill and plug the screw holes, and drive the screws if hook-on brackets are supplied.

Fig 120 Hook the cabinet fixing brackets over the wall screws and adjust the level to align individual units.

Fig 121 Hang and align successive units in the same way, then lock them all together with connector screws.

Fitting Worktops

Kitchen worktops are now almost all the post-formed variety, with the laminate surface having a gently curved front edge. The core is usually 35mm (1⅜in) thick chipboard, which can be very hard to cut – definitely a job for a power saw.

What to do

With all your base units in place, start by working out where you intend to have joints between lengths; on do-it-yourself kitchens these are generally covered by special cover strips. Then cut each run of worktop to length and lay it in position to check the fit. Secure it to the units by screwing up into its underside through brackets or joint blocks fitted inside the base units. Add the cover strips at each joint or change of direction before butting up and fixing the next length of worktop.

If you are fitting an inset hob or sink, mark its outline using the template provided and make the cut-out before you fit the worktop in place. Lay-on sinks simply sit on top of their base units.

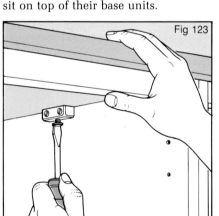

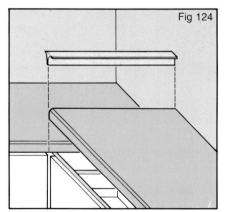

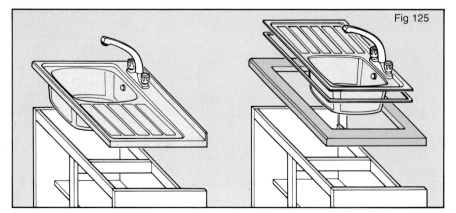

Fig 122 (*above*)
Worktops and sink units complete the installation of a fitted kitchen.

Fig 123 With all the base units in place, cut the worktops to length and lay them in place. Secure them to the units with brackets or joint blocks.

Fig 124 Use special profiled seals to link adjacent lengths of worktop.

Fig 125 Lay-on sink units simply sit on top of their base units and are held down with brackets. Inset sinks fit within cut-outs in the worktop, and must be bedded on sealing gaskets to prevent water seeping beneath them and saturating the worktop core.

Fitting Doors and Drawers

The final job when installing flat-pack kitchen or bedroom furniture is to attach and align the units' doors, and to make up and fit the drawers. Doors are hung on adjustable hinges, while drawers come in kit form and have to be assembled first.

What to do

The hinges used on almost all kitchen and bedroom units nowadays allow the doors to open to at least 135°, and incorporate three directions of adjustment to allow the doors to be perfectly aligned.

Start by fitting the hinge to its base section within the unit. Then loosen the base section's fixing screws to move the door up and down. Then adjust the two screws on the hinge mounting arm to move the door from side to side and in and out as necessary. Tighten up all the screws fully after making the adjustments.

Make up drawer kits by snapping the drawer sides together round the base, and then add the drawer front. False fronts may be adjustable for final alignment.

Fig 126 (*above*) Add doors and drawers once all the units are in place.

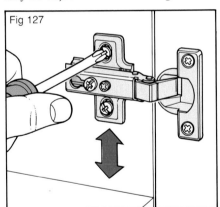

Fig 127

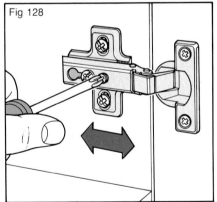

Fig 128

Fig 127 Cupboard doors are hung on adjustable lay-on hinges which allow the doors to be opened to beyond 90°. Secure the hinge arm to its baseplate and adjust the fixing screws to make the door hang at the correct level.

Fig 128 Use the adjuster screws to move the door face in or out so it closes smoothly and aligns correctly with its neighbours.

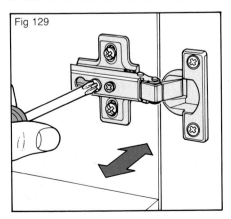

Fig 129

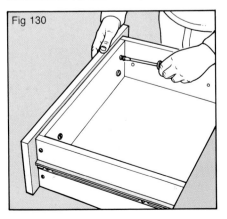

Fig 130

Fig 129 Make further adjustments as needed to prevent the door from fouling its partner as it closes.

Fig 130 Drawers usually come as kits which are simple to assemble. Screw on the false drawer fronts from within the drawer.

Fitting Door Locks

Good locks are essential if your front and back doors are to offer a secure barrier to would-be intruders. For security when you are out (and at night when you are asleep) you need a mortise lock recessed into the edge of the door. For convenience, fit a surface-mounted deadlatch as well; it is easier to operate than a mortise lock for opening and closing the door when you are in, and will provide a degree of extra security when you are not.

Any mortise locks you buy should be the five-lever type with a deadbolt – a bolt that cannot be pushed back by force when it has been locked with the key. The door stile into which the lock body is recessed must be at least 45mm (1¾in) thick; if it is not, fitting the lock will seriously weaken the door. Standard locks need a stile at least 75mm (3in) wide; narrow-stile locks are available for stiles 65mm (2½in) wide.

Surface-mounted locks (also known as cylinder locks) are also available in standard and narrow-stile versions, and some have high-security cylinders.

What to do: Mortise Locks

If you are replacing an existing lock, check whether you can buy a replacement that will fit the existing mortise. To remove the old lock, open the door, extend the bolt, undo the fixing screws in the lock faceplate and pull on the bolt with a self-grip wrench to remove the lock.

If you are fitting a new lock, place it in line with the main cross rail of the door. Offer up the lock body to the door edge so you can mark the height of the mortise on it. Mark out the mortise, drill out the bulk of the waste to the correct depth and clean up the hole with a chisel.

Next, slide the lock into place and mark round its faceplate on the door edge. Cut a shallow recess for the faceplate, then hold the lock against the door face so you can mark the holes for the spindle and key. Drill and saw these out, fit the lock and drive in the faceplate screws.

Extend the bolt so you can mark where it will meet the door frame, then cut a recess in the frame for the striking plate.

What you need:
- lock and keeper
- pencil
- tape measure
- try square
- drill plus wood bit
- chisel and mallet
- bradawl
- padsaw for keyhole
- screwdriver
- junior hacksaw

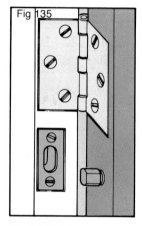

Fig 135

Fig 135 Fit hinge bolts for extra reinforcement along the hinged edge of the door.

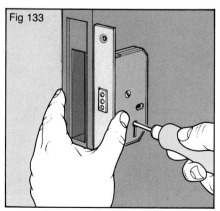

Fig 131

Fig 132

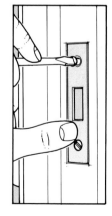

Fig 133

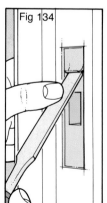

Fig 134

Fig 131 Use the lock body to mark the depth of the mortise on the door edge, then mark its width using a mortise gauge set to match the lock thickness.

Fig 132 Drill out the mortise to the correct depth, then square off the recess neatly with a chisel.

Fig 133 Chisel out a shallow recess to accept the lock faceplate, then mark the position of the keyhole. Cut it with a drill and padsaw, then fit the lock in place.

Fig 134 Close the door so you can mark the position of the keeper on the frame. Then chisel out the recess and fit the keeper.

Fitting Door Locks

What to do: Cylinder Locks

Although the lock body is mounted on the door surface, its locking mechanism is contained in a cylinder that fits in a 32mm (1¼in) diameter hole passing through the door. Start by using the template supplied with the lock to mark the position of this hole on the door face, then drill it out with a flat bit or hole saw. If the lock body has an endplate, cut a recess for it in the edge of the door.

Next, screw the lock backplate to the inner face of the door, insert the cylinder and drive the fixing screws through the backplate into the cylinder to lock it in place. Locate the lock body on the backplate with the connector bar in its slot (cut the bar with a hacksaw if it is too long), and screw it to the door.

Close the door so you can mark the position of the striking plate on the frame, then chisel a rebate for it and screw it securely into place.

Complete your door security by adding hinge bolts, a chain and a door viewer.

Fig 136 (*above*) Choose special narrow-stile locks for glazed doors.

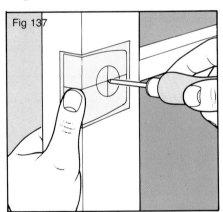

Fig 137 Use the paper template supplied with the lock to mark the position of the cylinder on the door, and drill out the hole.

Fig 138 Offer up the cylinder and screw the backplate to it.

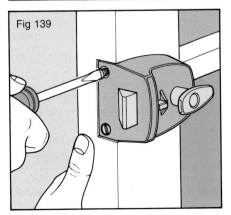

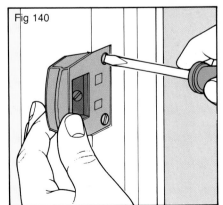

Fig 139 Cut the connector bar to length, locate the lock body over it and attach it to the door edge.

Fig 140 Mark the position of the keeper on the door frame, chisel out any recesses needed and then fit the keeper to the frame.

43

Fitting Window Locks

Windows are if anything even more vulnerable than external doors; in half of all domestic burglaries the window is the entry and/or the escape route for the intruder. The main reason is that most window catches are very easy to open by force, or after breaking a nearby pane of glass. The other problem is that people will leave windows open . . .

Only education will alter the latter bad habit, but fitting – and using – locks will prevent burglars from opening windows (few like climbing through broken panes). It may also help to reduce your household insurance premiums.

Most homes in this country have timber-framed windows and the security products available reflect this, being designed either for surface or flush-mounting. However, there are several locks specifically designed for metal-framed windows, including sliding patio types. The most convenient are those that lock automatically when the window is closed – useful if you are forgetful – while the most secure are those that are key-operated.

What to do: Casement Windows

You have several choices of lock for securing side-hinged casement windows and their top-hinged vents. For timber windows the most secure and least obtrusive are mortise rack bolts which are set into the edge of the casement and when operated (with a special fluted key) shoot a bolt into a recess in the frame. Fit them in pairs, one near the top and one near the bottom of the casement.

An alternative, which can also be used for top vents, is the two-part frame lock. This is surface-mounted and is operated by pushing the spring-loaded bolt into its keeper when the window is closed. It needs a key to open it. Again, fit two on tall casements, just one on top vents.

You can also fit locking window catches in place of the existing ones, and secure window stays with stay locks.

Note that all these surface-mounted devices are only as secure as the screws holding them in place, so fit longer screws than those supplied for extra strength.

What you need:
Casement windows:
- surface-mounted push-locks plus bradawl and screwdriver *or*
- locking cockspur handle plus bradawl and screwdriver *or*
- mortise rack bolts plus power drill with twist and wood bits, pencil, chisel, bradawl and screwdriver *or*
- casement stay locks plus bradawl and screwdriver

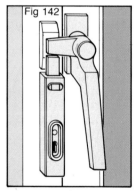

Fig 142 On metal windows, fit surface-mounted cockspur locks.

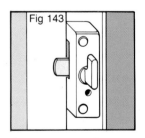

Fig 143 An alternative for metal windows is to use special frame locks.

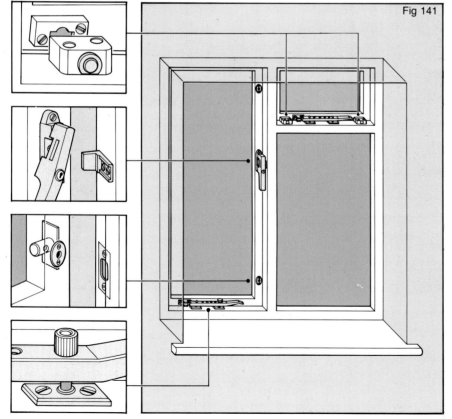

Fig 141

Fig 141 Secure opening casements and top lights with surface-mounted push locks, locking cockspur handles, recessed mortise rack bolts or casement stay locks.

Fitting Window Locks

What to do: Sash Windows

The simplest way of improving the security of a timber sliding sash window is to replace the existing centre catch with a locking type. However, it is advisable to add additional security devices — ideally in pairs at each side of the window.

The most secure and least obtrusive lock is the dual screw — a threaded bolt that passes through a metal barrel in the top rail of the inner sash into a receiver in the bottom rail of the outer one. To fit it you simply drill a 10mm (⅜in) hole and tap the barrel into place, then turn in the screw with a special key.

An alternative is the surface-mounted push bolt, which is fitted on the top rail of the inner sash so its spring-loaded bolt fits in a hole in the side rail of the outer sash. If you want some ventilation as well as improved security, fit pairs of window stops. Some have pegs which you insert when you want to lock the window; more secure types have a recessed spring-loaded bolt which you release with a key.

Fig 144 Provide extra security for patio doors and horizontally sliding windows by fitting screw-on push locks.

> **What you need:**
> *Sash windows:*
> - acorn stops plus bradawl and screwdriver *or*
> - surface-mounted push-locks plus drill with wood bit, bradawl and screwdriver *or*
> - locking fitch plus bradawl and screwdriver *or*
> - dual screws plus drill with twist drill and screwdriver

Fig 145 Secure sliding sash windows with acorn stops, push locks, locking centre catches or dual screws. Acorn stops allow the window to be locked with the window slightly open for ventiliation. Fit all types except locking catches in pairs.

Fig 145

45

Hanging a New Door

Replacing a door is likely to involve a wider range of your woodworking skills than many other DIY projects. For a start, you may have to reduce the size of any off-the-peg door you buy to make it fit its frame. You will then have to chisel recesses for the hinges and fit these to the door edge, and finally you will have to fit a lock or latch and other door furniture.

The type of door you choose for a particular location will be dependent mainly on its appearance; remember, however, that exterior doors need to be stronger and thicker than interior ones. All come in a range of standard sizes (see CHECK); if the door you are replacing is not a standard size, select the nearest larger size.

Provided that the existing hinges are sound and in good working order, there is no reason why you should not re-use them to hang the new door, unless it is significantly heavier than the one it is replacing. You may also want to retain existing door furniture for re-use on the new door. However, it is generally a good idea to fit a new latch or lock mechanism.

What to do

Start by removing the existing door and its hinges (unless these are to be re-used). You may have to chip paint out of the screw slots and apply heat (from a soldering iron, for example) to shift stubborn screws. Check its measurements so you know exactly how much (if anything) will have to be removed from the height or width of the new door. You can safely remove up to 20mm (¾in) from the sides, top or bottom of a panelled door without weakening it, but you should not remove more than about 10mm (⅜in) from any edge of a flush door. The door should have 3mm (⅛in) clearance between it and its frame at the top and down the sides, and 6mm (¼in) clearance at floor level.

If you have to reduce the size of the door, use a plane or a power planer to remove amounts up to about 6mm (¼in), and a saw for larger amounts. Remove equal amounts from opposite edges to avoid weakening one stile unduly, and to maintain the symmetry of panelled doors.

What you need:
- new door and hinges
- latch or lock
- door knobs
- tape measure
- panel or jig saw
- pencil or marking knife
- chisel
- timber wedges
- bradawl
- screwdriver
- drill plus wood bits for latch/lock mortise and spindle/keyhole

CHECK
- whether your existing door is a standard size. Common sizes for front doors are 2032 × 813mm (6ft 8in × 2ft 8in), 1981 × 838mm (6ft 6in × 2ft 9in) and 1981 × 762mm (6ft 6in × 2ft 6in). The last two are also the commonest for room doors, but a range of other sizes is generally available.

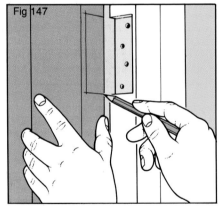

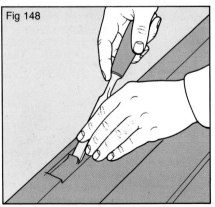

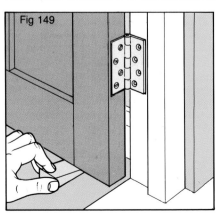

Fig 146 Many doors are sold with projecting stiles to prevent corner damage in storage. Saw these off before you start to fit the door.

Fig 147 Stand the door against the frame with scrap timber under its bottom edge to give adequate floor clearance and mark the position of the hinge recesses on the door edge.

Fig 148 Chisel out the hinge recesses to a depth that matches the thickness of the hinge leaf, and screw the hinges to the door.

Fig 149 Stand the door against the frame, again wedged up to the correct level to clear the floor. Use a portable workbench to hold it in position if you do not have a helper.

Hanging a New Door

Offer the hinged edge of the door up to the frame (get someone to support it for you, or use the jaws of your portable workbench to hold it) and mark the existing hinge positions on the door edge. Use your hinges as templates to mark out the hinge recesses, and cut them carefully with a sharp chisel. Then fit the hinges.

Next, support the door as before with wedges under the bottom edge so you can drive the screws securing the hinges into the existing recesses on the door frame. If they do not grip tightly, drive slim glued dowels or wood offcuts into the screw holes and drill fresh pilot holes for the screws.

Check that the door swings freely and closes properly. Then mark the position of the latch against the existing striking plate on the door frame, and drill a hole into the door edge to accept the latch mechanism. Next, cut a shallow recess in the door edge to accommodate the latch faceplate, mark and drill a hole through the door for the spindle and screw the latch mechanism into place. Finally, fit the spindle and add the door knobs.

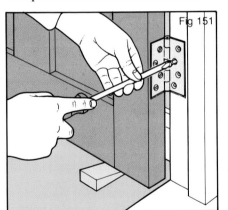

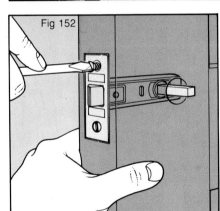

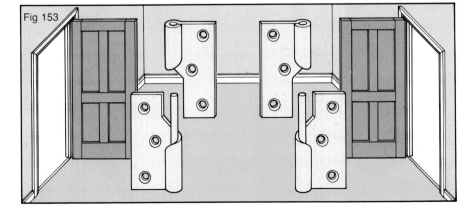

Fig 150 (*above*) Hanging new doors can transform a room's appearance.

Fig 151 Screw the hinges to the frame, ensuring that the screw heads fit flush in their countersinks.

Fig 152 With the door hung, close it so you can mark the latch position to line up with the existing keeper on the door frame. Drill a hole for the latch body, cut a recess for its faceplate and drill a hole for the spindle, then secure the latch in place and fit the door handles.

Fig 153 Fit rising butt hinges to lift the door clear of carpets. Note that these are 'handed' according to which way the door is to open.

Fitting Sliding Doors

If your house is short of space, or you have traffic areas such as halls and landings where clashing doors are a problem, you will appreciate the advantages that a sliding door has to offer. It needs just a clear wall space next to it, roughly equal to its own width, against which it slides as it opens.

However, you have to weigh the space-saving and safety aspects of these doors against their drawbacks. For a start, they are more difficult to draughtproof than ordinary hinged doors, although some sliding door gears are designed specifically to counter·this problem by moving the door in tight against the door jambs as it closes. Secondly, you will have to modify the door frame to install the door. In addition, you might have to reposition fixtures such as radiators and surface-mounted light switches and power points near the door. Lastly, because you have to buy special gears to hang these door, the installation is likely to prove a little more expensive than if you were hanging the door on conventional hinges.

What to do

Generally speaking, any type of door can be used for a sliding door installation. Flush doors are the most likely choice, but there is no reason why a panelled type should not be used if it suits your decor. However, remember that when converting a hinged door to sliding action, you will need a new, larger door unless you are prepared to modify the existing frame.

To operate sliding doors, you need the right door gear. For sliding room doors there is a wide choice, all broadly similar in principle. A track is screwed to the face of the wall above the door opening, and wheeled runners attached to the top edge of the door itself run along the track as the door slides. There are usually two runners per door. More expensive types, often described as 'silent', have a complete carriage bar that runs almost the full width of the door, and which may run on ball bearings rather than wheels. In either case, the track is usually concealed behind a plain or decorative pelmet.

What you need:
- new door
- door track kit to match door size
- batten for mounting door track on wall
- old chisel or other lever for removing top architrave section
- tenon saw for trimming tops of side architrave sections
- drill plus twist and masonry drill bits
- screws and wallplugs
- screwdriver
- spirit level
- hacksaw
- pair of spanners

CHECK
- that your new door is wide enough to cover the existing door opening
- that the door gear is suitable for the weight of door being hung; solid doors need heavy-duty track
- that the door bottom will easily clear floor coverings

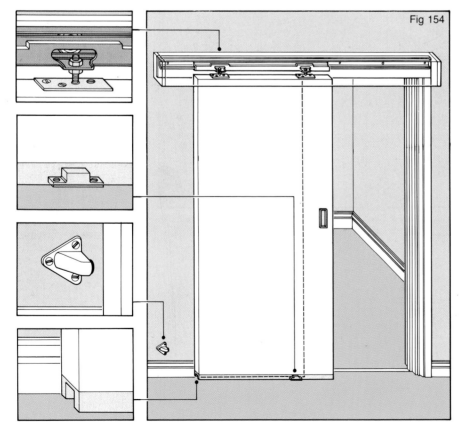

Fig 154

Fig 154 A sliding door needs an area of clear wall against which it slides when open. The track is fitted to a wall batten above the door opening, and can be concealed with a pelmet. The hangers allow the door level to be adjusted, and floor guides keep it on line. A door stop prevents it from running off the track when opened.

Fitting Sliding Doors

The sequence of operations for installing a sliding room door varies slightly from manufacturer to manufacturer, so it is important to follow to the letter the fitting instructions supplied with the gear. Generally speaking, the sequence most manufacturers recommend is as follows.

Remove and cut back the door architrave, and screw a batten — long enough to carry the door track — to the wall. Next, attach the door hangers to the top edge or face of the door, and offer up the door so you can mark the height at which the track should be fixed to the wall batten. Fix the track to the batten, checking that it is horizontal with your spirit level.

Attach the runners to the door hangers, hang the door on the track and adjust the hangers so the door is level and clears the floor adequately. Fit the floor guide(s) and door stop. Finally, add filler pieces to the door frame and/or the door's trailing edge to give a neater appearance and help to stop draughts, and fit a pelmet to the wall batten if you want to conceal the track and hangers.

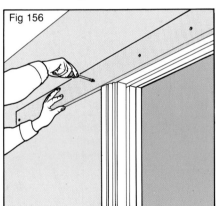

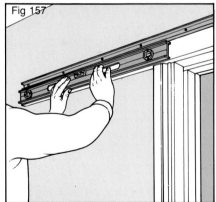

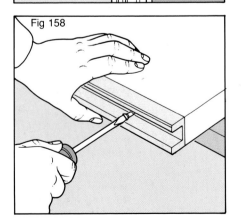

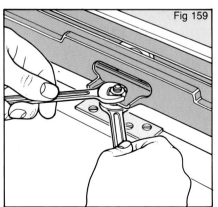

Fig 155 (*above*) Sliding doors are an excellent choice if space or access is restricted.

Fig 156 Remove the architrave above the door opening and fit a wall batten long enough to carry the door track.

Fig 157 Screw the track to the batten and check that it is level.

Fig 158 Cut the door down to the correct height if necessary and fit the guide channel to its bottom edge.

Fig 159 Fit the hangers and bottom guide, and hang the door on the track. Adjust the hangers so it hangs squarely and opens and closes smoothly.

Fitting Skirtings and Architraves

Skirting boards are fitted to plastered walls at ground level to protect the plaster surface from damage by careless feet or furniture. Until recently, the fashion was for fairly low, plain skirting boards with either a pencil rounded or splayed-and-rounded cross-section; these were usually painted. However, many people are now replacing these with deeper, more ornate skirtings in traditional profiles such as torus or ogee, often stained and varnished instead of being given a painted finish.

The smaller types are generally cut from 150 × 19mm (6 × ¾in) timber, but more ornate styles may be up to 225mm (9in) high and are generally 25mm (1in) thick. Some skirtings are now machined with a different profile on each face; they are known as double-sided, and you use whichever face you prefer.

If you are trying to match existing period skirtings and cannot find an exact replacement, you can often create an acceptable match by topping flat planks with decorative beadings of various types.

Architraves perform a similar job to skirtings, being fitted round flush door and window openings to create a decorative and protective border. They are available in styles to match both plain and ornate skirtings, and are either run down to floor level (with the skirting abutting their outer edges) or rest on a small floor-level plinth block.

Dados and picture rails are mouldings that are 'planted' on wall surfaces, the former at waist height and the latter about 600mm (24in) below ceiling level. They were both popular from Victorian times until the 1930s, and are now making a comeback. The dado was designed to protect the plaster from damage by carelessly-moved furniture, and also provides a natural break in the wall's colour scheme; traditionally, the area below the dado might be panelled or finished in Lincrusta, while that above it would be papered or painted. The picture rail allows pictures to be hung – and moved about – at will, and also provides a visual break in rooms with high ceilings.

What you need:
- cold chisel plus scrap timber to protect wall
- claw hammer
- replacement battens for skirting fixings
- masonry nails
- oval wire nails
- new skirting *or* architrave mouldings
- pencil *or* marking knife
- tenon saw
- jig saw for mitred joints and corners
- coping saw for butt joints
- drill plus twist and masonry bits
- screws and wallplugs
- screwdriver

TIP
When fitting skirting boards round external angles, cut the mitres so that the boards meet at an angle of just less than 90°. This ensures that the joint will not open up after fixing.

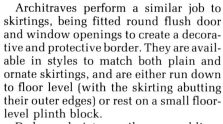

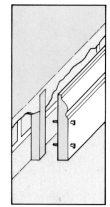
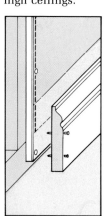
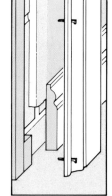

Fig 160 Skirting boards in older homes are usually fixed to timber grounds that are either nailed to the brickwork or wedged into it, while in newer buildings they are generally nailed direct to the wall surface. Architraves are pinned to the door frame.

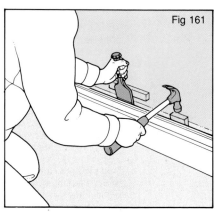

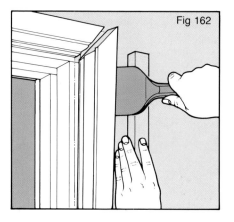

Fig 161 To remove a length of skirting for replacement, lever it away from the wall with a brick bolster or crowbar (using packing to protect the plaster) and drive in wedges to help pull the board off right along its length.

Fig 162 Use a similar levering technique to remove lengths of door architrave.

Fitting Skirtings and Architraves

What to do

Existing skirtings and architraves are almost always nailed in place, so are generally easy to prise off and remove. In older homes, the skirtings are generally fixed to timber blocks nailed to the wall, while in newer ones they may be fixed directly with masonry nails. Remove the old boards by levering them away from the wall carefully, driving in timber wedges as you proceed. Replace the timber blocks if they are damaged. Then cut the new length of skirting, mitring external corners and scribing internal ones, and nail it into place. On timber-framed walls, try to drive the fixing nails into the timber uprights of the frame.

Architraves are nailed directly to the edges of the door frame. Prise them off carefully after running a knife down the edge abutting the frame to break the paint line, then cut new pieces to length and nail them into place.

Attach picture and dado rails with screws and wallplugs rather than nails.

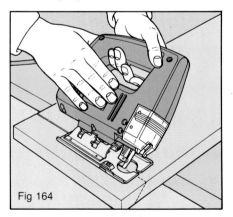

Fig 164

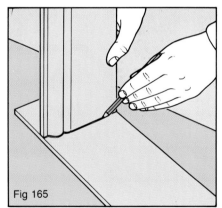

Fig 165

Fig 163 (*above*) Skirting and dado rails not only finish off a room's decor; they also help protect the plaster from accidental damage.

Fig 164 Use a jigsaw to make the 45° cuts for external corners.

Fig 165 Form butt joints at internal corners. Scribe the board's profile onto one of the lengths and cut it with a coping saw.

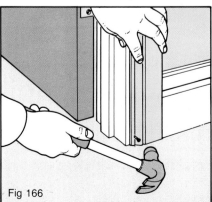

Fig 166

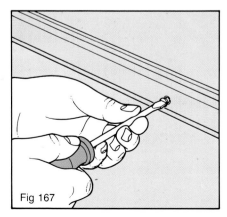

Fig 167

Fig 166 Architraves usually run down to floor level. Mitre the top corner joints and nail the lengths to the door frame.

Fig 167 Fit picture and dado rails with screws and wallplugs rather than using masonry nails.

Fitting a New Balustrade

The balustrades that guard stairs and landings are built up by setting individual balusters along the edge of the flight and round the landing perimeter, and topping them with a continuous handrail which runs between the main structural supports of the staircase – the newel posts. In many homes, previous owners have taken dreadful liberties with the original balustrade, often removing the mouldings, painting them so carelessly that all the detail is now obscured, or cladding them with materials such as hardboard. So long as the staircase itself is sound, one of the most rewarding improvement projects is to install a completely new balustrade.

Thanks to the arrival of kits containing replacement mouldings, extension newel posts and handrails, plus all the fittings needed to put them together, it is a simple job to remove the existing balustrade and build up a new one. Turned mouldings in a range of woods are the most popular choice, or you can select plainer mouldings if that suits the design and style of your staircase more.

What to do

Start by deciding which kit you want to install, then study the manufacturer's literature carefully so you can estimate your requirements correctly. You have to measure the length of each section of the balustrade, and then follow the guidelines on baluster spacing (to satisfy the requirements of the Building Regulations they must be fixed close enough to prevent a 100mm (4in) sphere from passing between them) so you can work out how many will be needed for each section. That will in turn dictate how many infill fillets and fixing brackets you require.

To dismantle the existing balustrade, start by removing any cladding covering the balusters, then saw through these and wrench out the cut sections. Lever out the pinned-on timber fillets between the balusters. Next, cut through the handrails next to the newel posts (use a hacksaw if you hit hidden metal fixings) and lift them away. Finally, saw off the newel posts if these are also being replaced. Follow the

What you need:
- newel posts plus post caps
- handrails
- balusters
- string capping
- baluster spacers
- handrail brackets
- tape measure
- claw hammer
- try square
- panel saw
- power drill plus large wood bit
- sliding bevel
- tenon saw
- screwdriver
- spirit level
- woodworking adhesive
- oval wire nails

CHECK
- that you measure up the length of handrail required carefully to ensure accuracy.
- that balusters are spaced with gaps no larger than 100mm (4in) between them.
- that handrails are between 840mm and 1m (2ft 9in and 3ft 3in) above the line of the stair nosings.

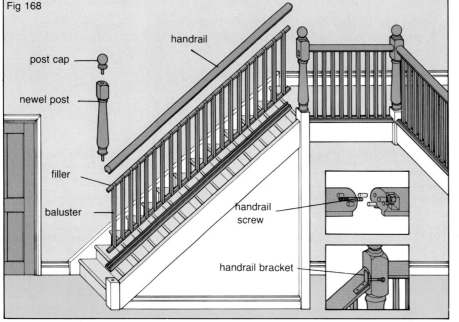

Fig 168

- post cap
- newel post
- handrail
- filler
- baluster
- handrail screw
- handrail bracket

Fig 168 Complete kits of stairparts allow you to form new handrails on staircases and round landings. Newel post extensions are dowel-jointed to the cut-down post stubs, then the new rail is fitted and the balusters set in place. Specially designed fittings connect the rails to the posts and also join long lengths of rail together.

Fitting a New Balustrade

kit manufacturer's instructions about precisely where to make the cut, and ensure that it is square by first marking a cutting line all round the post.

Now you can start building up the new balustrade. It is usual to fit the newel post extensions first, using glue and a large-diameter wooden dowel. Check that each is truly vertical as you fit it. Then add capping mouldings to receive the baluster feet if these are part of the kit, and cut and fit each length of handrail in place using a sliding bevel or a paper template to mark the correct cutting angle on the ends of each length. Make sure that all fixings are secure at this stage.

Check that the rails are parallel with the capping mouldings, then start fitting the baluster mouldings. Again use a sliding bevel or template to mark the cutting angle; so it matches the slope of the handrail, then slide each baluster into place after fitting the spacer fillet between it and its neighbour. Nail the head of each baluster to the underside of the handrail if spacer fillets are not used here.

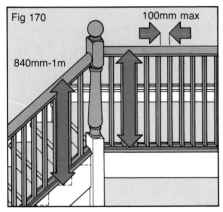

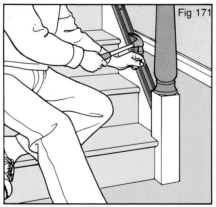

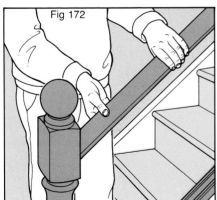

Fig 169 (*above*)
Replacing an old handrail and balustrade can give an existing staircase a dramatic facelift.

Fig 170 The handrail must be between 840mm (2ft 9in) and 1m (3ft 3in) high, measured from the line of the tread nosings, and the gaps between the individual balusters must not exceed 100mm (4in).

Fig 171 Fit the newel post extension, then add the capping rail to the staircase's open string.

Fig 172 Measure, cut and fit the various handrail sections next.

Fig 173 Complete the job by cutting the balusters to length, with their ends angled to match the slope of the staircase, and secure them in place before fitting the spacers.

53

Cladding Walls

Wooden panelling of one sort or another has been a popular way of decorating interior walls for centuries. It is good-looking, hard-wearing and warm to the touch, and can be crafted and finished in several different ways. One of the most popular effects is the use of tongued-and-grooved boards. Softwood, often described as 'knotty pine', is the obvious choice, but other more exotic woods can be used instead.

Apart from its looks, cladding has other advantages. For a start, it is the perfect cover-up for walls with defective (or missing) plaster. It feels warm to the touch, so helps to cut down condensation, and if insulation is fitted behind it the result is a much warmer room – a particular boon in properties with solid walls which are difficult to insulate. Lastly, it can help to reduce noise transmission between rooms. The only drawback is that the room is made slightly smaller, and some re-positioning of fittings such as wall lights, switches and power points may be necessary.

What to do

Start fixing battens at the top and sides of the wall to be clad, and at floor level if you have removed the skirting. Then add inter-mediate battens at about 600mm (24in) intervals across the wall, and fix short lengths of batten round switch or socket mounting boxes.

Cut the first board to length and offer it up to one edge of the area to be clad with the grooved edge in the corner. Use a spirit level to ensure that it is vertical, then scribe the profile of the side wall and its skirting board onto its face. Use a jigsaw to cut along the marked line, then nail it to the battens with panel pins driven at an angle through the exposed tongue. Add another pin driven into each batten through the face of the board.

Fix the second board by sliding its grooved edge over the tongue of the first board. Then drive pins through its tongue as before. Repeat this process to fix all the other full-length boards to the battens. Leave the last length, which will have to

What you need:
- cladding
- scotia beading and new skirting boards
- oval wire nails or secret fixing clips
- tape measure
- spirit level
- pencil
- fixing battens
- masonry nails or screws and wallplugs
- try square
- tenon saw or jigsaw
- hammer
- pin punch
- plane or Surform

CHECK
- that cladding boards are not warped or split, are free from dead knots which may fall out, and have broadly the same overall colour and grain pattern.

TIP
Condition the boards indoors for several days before fixing them in place to avoid shrinkage as the boards dry out.

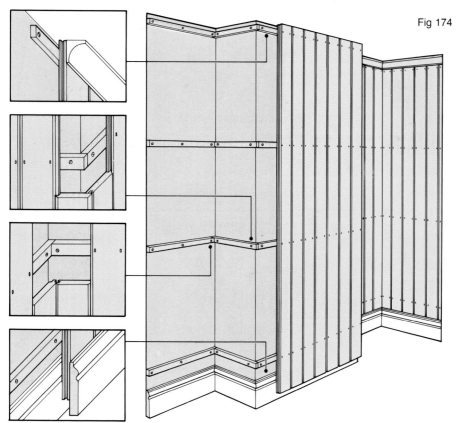

Fig 174

Fig 174 Tongued-and-grooved timber cladding is secured to horizontal wall battens at floor and ceiling level and at roughly 750mm (2ft 6in) intervals in between. Cut the boards to leave a narrow air gap at the ceiling and floor; these are covered by lengths of scotia beading and new skirting board. Form butt joints at internal and external corners, with the exposed board edge planed smooth at external corners for a neat finish.

54

be scribed to fit, until later. To fix cladding round a light switch or socket outlet, make small cut-outs in the boards that will fit over them using a coping saw, pad saw or power jigsaw.

At internal corners, the last length must be scribed and cut down to width. Pin or hold it on top of the last whole board fitted, and use an offcut of cladding to scribe the wall profile back onto the board. Cut along the scribed line, offer the board up into position and fix it to the battens with pins driven through the board face and punched just below the board surface. Fill the punch holes.

However carefully you work, the cut ends of the boards will always look a little ragged. Neaten them off by adding slim quadrant beading at ceiling and wall edges, and replace the skirting board at floor level. With all the boards and trims in place, sand the wall surface down lightly and wipe the board surfaces down with a clean, lint-free cloth dampened with white spirit to remove dust, ready for the final finish to be applied.

Fig 175 (*above*) Timber cladding gives a room a warm, natural appearance.

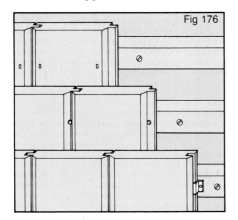

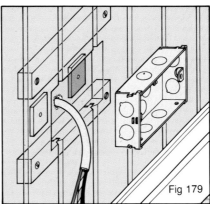

Fig 176 You can fix the cladding to the wall battens in one of three ways – by nailing through the board face, by secret nailing through the tongues or by using proprietary fixing clips.

Fig 177 At internal corners, scribe the edge of the last board so it matches the profile of the side wall.

Fig 178 At window reveals, finish the cladding neatly with a corner batten.

Fig 179 Reposition flush wiring accessories so their faceplates finish flush with the cladding.

Building a Partition Wall

Few homes make the best use of their available floor space, and few families fit perfectly into the space allotted to them, especially as they expand. One solution to this problem is to subdivide existing rooms, by building timber-framed partition walls. Obviously you can do this only if the original room is of a reasonable size, but especially in many older properties there is often plenty of scope for manoeuvre.

When you are planning this job, you need to give careful thought to the siting of the wall. The newly-partitioned room must have a separate window if it is to be a habitable room (a bedroom or living room); you are not allowed to run walls up to the centre of existing windows. In other rooms – for example, a new bathroom – you do not need a window so long as you provide mechanical ventilation. The new room will also need access; for bedrooms this should ideally *not* be through an existing room, so you may have to plan a new access corridor to the new room. You will also need to think about re-routing plumbing or wiring and repositioning or adding radiators.

What to do

Once you have decided on the precise position of the new wall, you can start on the actual construction. Although it may appear to be a big job, it is in fact an extremely simple one in carpentry terms; so long as you can measure accurately and cut squarely you cannot go wrong.

Start by screwing the headplate in place across the room. Prop it up against the ceiling while you make the fixings – directly into the ceiling joists if the plate runs at right angles to them, or to timber noggings fixed between the joists if it runs parallel to them and you cannot site it directly under the joist. Then drop a plumb line at each end, nail the soleplate to the floor and add the vertical timbers at each end of the wall, securing them with screws driven into wallplugs. Check at this stage that the basic framework is vertical and correctly aligned.

Next, mark the positions of the studs on the soleplate; it is usual to set them at 400mm (16in) centres so that the edges of

What you need:
- 100 × 50mm (4 × 2in) sawn softwood for the wall framing
- plasterboard
- new skirting and architrave mouldings
- new door plus fittings and door furniture
- tape measure
- panel or jigsaw
- spirit level
- plumb bob and line
- screws and screwdriver
- claw hammer and round wire nails
- plasterboard nails

Fig 180 A timber stud partition consists of a row of vertical studs nailed into place between a ceiling-mounted headplate and a floor-mounted soleplate.

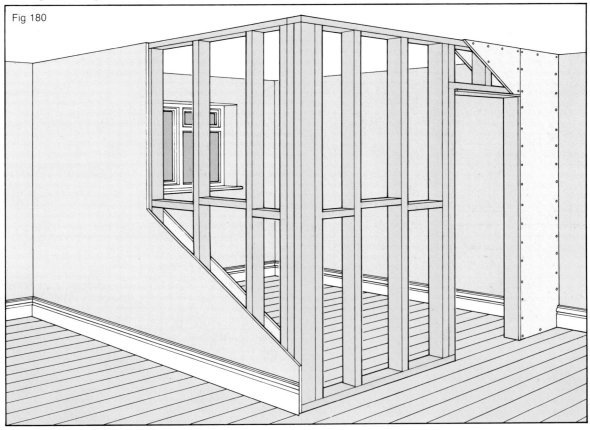

Fig 180

Building a Partition Wall

standard sheets of plasterboard meet over the centre line of the studs. Also mark the door position and cut away a section of the soleplate at this point.

Prop the first stud in place and skew-nail it to the head- and soleplates. Check that it is vertical. Then add more studs in turn, working along the wall. Where the partition turns a corner, add an extra stud to fill in the angle where the two walls meet. Then use shorter lengths to form door openings, and complete the framework by adding horizontal noggings, skew-nailed into place between the studs to create a strong, rigid framework.

If wiring or pipework need to run through the wall, fit this next. Run cables and supply pipes through holes drilled in the studs, and cut notches for waste pipes. Mount battens between the studs to support flush wiring accessories.

Finally, start nailing up the plasterboard sheets to both sides of the wall, fitting them tightly up against the ceiling and leaving a slight gap at floor level; this will be covered by the skirting board.

Fig 181 (*above*) Building a stud partition wall does not require any great carpentry skills, just the ability to measure things accurately.

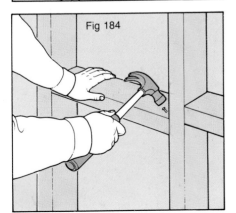

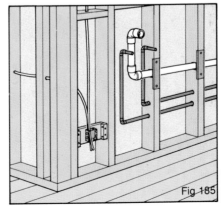

Fig 182 Use studs to prop the headplate in place while you fix it to the ceiling.

Fig 183 Skew nail the studs to the head and soleplates at 400mm (16in) centres.

Fig 184 Add noggings between the studs.

Fig 185 Mount wiring accessories and run in plumbing pipes before cladding the wall.

Sanding Floorboards

Many homes have suspended timber floors, consisting of closely-butted or tongued-and-grooved boards nailed to joists, and cleaning them up so they can be left exposed is a popular project especially in older properties. So long as the boards are intrinsically sound and have not shrunk unduly, the resulting floor surface can make an extremely attractive feature.

What to do

Start by assessing whether the floor needs major cosmetic treatment; you may need to lift and re-lay the boards to close up large gaps, or to reverse seriously damaged boards so their undamaged undersides are uppermost. Then punch down all the fixing nails ready for sanding to begin.

Hire a power floor sander and a smaller edging sander from a plant hire shop, and make sure you have a good supply of abrasive sheets in various grades. Sand the floor diagonally first to remove the worst soiling, then run the sander parallel to the boards before finishing the edges.

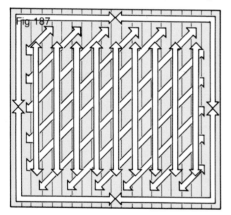

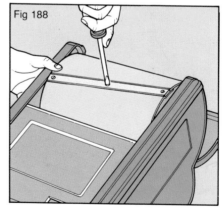

Fig 186 (*above*) Sanded and sealed floorboards make a stunning floor surface.

Fig 187 The correct sanding sequence is diagonal runs first, then runs along the board direction, followed by edge sanding.

Fig 188 Make sure the sanding sheets are properly secured to the sanding drum.

Fig 189 Use coarse, medium and then fine abrasives in turn, finishing off by sanding along the boards.

Fig 190 Sand the edges of the room and other awkward to reach areas using the edge sander.

OUTDOOR JOBS

As far as woodworking is concerned, there is rather less scope for exercising your skills out of doors than there is inside the house. There is of course the endless battle to keep the elements from attacking your outdoor woodwork – window frames, doors, fences, gates and so on – but this is routine maintenance work rather than being a genuine home improvement, and is dealt with in the next chapter. However, there are also several outdoor woodworking projects you could undertake that are all well within the capabilities of the average householder, and are worth doing yourself instead of calling in a professional.

What you can tackle

Most of the commonest outdoor woodworking projects concern jobs such as putting up fences, hanging gates and erecting flat-pack outbuildings such as garden sheds and summerhouses, but there is one job you can carry out on the house itself which will save you a great deal of money.

Replacing windows Wood is by far the commonest material used for making window frames, and many homes have one or more windows so ravaged by rot that complete replacement is often the only solution to the problem. Unfortunately, over the last twenty years or so wooden windows have acquired a very poor track record, largely thanks to bad design and the use of poor-quality timber. Modern high-performance windows are a great improvement, however; they are made from good timber adequately treated with preservatives, and are well designed to operate efficiently and exclude the weather by having double-glazing and integral weather-stripping. Fitting one in place of an existing window is usually quite straightforward and the job should be comfortably completed inside a day unless there are unforeseen complications.

Building a shed There is nothing to stop you tackling the design and construction of your garden buildings, but you will get a better bargain by erecting prefabricated ones. Most suppliers offer a range of styles, shapes and sizes, and include everything you need to complete the assembly using a few simple tools.

Building a porch One project well worth considering involves using off-the-shelf window and door frames, topped off with a simple flat roof, to construct a porch outside your front or back door. There is a little more woodwork involved than in building a shed, but you have the advantage of being able to tailor-make it precisely to suit your requirements.

Fences and gates Putting up fences and gates is a classic do-it-yourself project; the materials are widely available, and little skill is needed to get good results and to make considerable savings on professional labour charges.

Fig 191 (*above*) Outdoor jobs range from simple tasks such as putting up trellis on garden walls to more complicated jobs like replacing window frames or building a garden shed.

Replacing a Wooden Window

If you have timber-framed windows that have been extensively damaged by rot, it is a relatively simple (and economical) job to replace them. Window manufacturers offer a huge range of off-the-shelf frames in a wide range of standard sizes and a number of different styles, so you should have little difficulty in finding one to match the window concerned. Try to choose high-performance types if possible, since these will not only perform well in use; they will also outlast cheaper types.

One difficulty you may encounter when trying to find an exact replacement is that windows are now made to metric sizes, while your existing windows are likely to have been made to fractionally larger imperial sizes. If this is the case, buy the closest match you can find, and be prepared to fill the small gap that will be left between frame and masonry by adding timber packing to the edges of the frame.

If your windows are non-standard sizes, you will have little option but to commission a local carpenter to make up a matching replacement for you.

What to do

Once you have obtained your replacement window, spend some time in preparation before you start work so you can complete the job and leave the house secure and weatherproof by the end of the day. If the frame is factory-primed ready for painting, apply either undercoat or the first of two topcoats; if it is to be stained, put on two coats of stain. Unless it has come complete with sealed-unit double-glazing, measure up and order the glass so you can glaze it as soon as it is fitted. Buy a sheet of heavy-duty polythene big enough to cover the frame, in case you are held up with the job for any reason.

To remove the old window frame, start by unscrewing opening casements and top lights if you can. Then put masking tape over the fixed glass and break it carefully so you can remove the shards. Dispose of them safely. Now you can saw through and remove the mullions and transoms (the vertical and horizontal dividers within the frame), followed by the frame sides

What you need:
- screwdriver
- hammer
- masking tape
- stout gloves
- panel saw
- crowbar
- club hammer and brick bolster
- new window frame
- filler strips or bench plane/Surform
- DPC strip
- spirit level
- drill plus twist and masonry drill bits
- frame fixings
- exterior mastic
- glass and putty

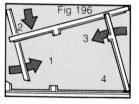

Fig 196 Lever the cut sections of the old frame out in sequence.

Fig 192 Start by unscrewing hinged casements and top lights from the frame, then carefully break and remove any fixed glass. Start the removal job by sawing through mullions and transoms.

Fig 193 Next, make saw cuts through the frame close to the corners so you can prise out the severed frame sections with a crowbar.

Fig 194 Use a brick bolster and club hammer to clean mortar or filler from the sides of the recess so you can check the precise size of the opening.

Fig 195 If the frame is slightly under size, pin packing strips on round the perimeter. Plane the frame down if it is fractionally too big.

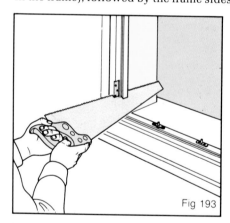

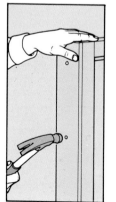

Replacing a Wooden Window

themselves. Use a crowbar to lever them away from the masonry, then remove any old fixings that remain and clean up the opening ready for the new window frame to be inserted. Check that the damp-proof course (DPC) beneath the opening is intact.

Now offer the new window up into position, using wedges to hold it while you check that it is standing vertically and square to the masonry. If the frame is fractionally shallower than the height of the opening, pack it up against the underside of the lintel with wedges.

When you are happy with its positioning, drill holes through the frame at each side of the window, switch to a masonry drill bit and drill on into the wall. Then insert special frame fixings – wallplugs plus screws with extra-long shanks – and tighten the screws to secure the frame in place. Use two fixings per side for windows up to 1.2m (4ft) high, three per side for taller windows.

Now all that remains is to weatherproof round the frame with mastic and set the glass or glazing units in place.

Fig 198

Fig 199

Fig 197 (*above*) Use wedges to hold the frame in place.

Fig 198 Lay a damp-proof course on the sill.

Fig 199 Check that the frame is vertical.

Fig 200 Drill holes and insert frame plugs. Tighten the screws.

Fig 201 Seal the frame with a bead of mastic.

Fig 200

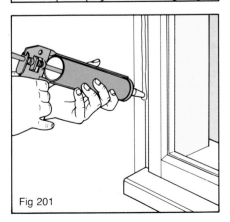

Fig 201

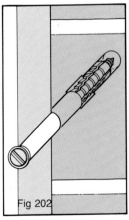

Fig 202

Fig 202 Frame plug.

Putting up a Shed

If you want a shed to keep your garden tools safe and tidy, or a summerhouse that will hold all your garden furniture, you can of course design and build one from scratch to suit your requirements. However, with the price of timber as high as it is today this is likely to be a very expensive way of tackling the project, and a better solution is generally to buy a prefabricated building from a local supplier. He gets his wood much more cheaply than you can because he buys in bulk, and his designs will be tried and tested so you can be sure that everything will fit together easily.

Most firms make sheds and summer-houses in modular sizes, from about 1.8 × 1.2m (6 × 4ft) upwards, so it should not be difficult to find the size you want in a style you like. Roofs are either ridged or pent (slightly sloping) and finished with roofing felt, while doors and windows may be sited in the side or end walls. Better-quality buildings have tongued-and-grooved walls, while cheaper types usually use shiplap or plain weatherboard planks.

What to do

Once you have selected the outbuilding you want, the first step is to prepare a suitable base for it. You can stand it on any existing hard surface – concrete, paving and so on – or lay a new concrete slab for it. Make this 75mm (3in) thick and a little larger than the building itself, and let it harden for three or four days before attempting to build on it.

Most buildings come with a timber floor, and it is wise to protect this from rot (even though it should be pre-treated with preservative) by resting its joists on strips of damp-proof course (DPC) material laid on the slab. Check that it is level, then get a helper to offer up the first wall panel to the floor edge. Brace it upright and manoeuvre the next wall panel into position. Check that the two are square to each other, then bolt, screw or nail them together. Bolts are better than other fixings at resisting damage caused by high winds; add them later if the shed you have bought is only nailed together.

What you need:
- prefabricated shed kit
- glass and putty for windows (not usually supplied)
- suitable base
- DPC strip material for use beneath timber floors
- hammer and nails or
- screwdriver and wood screws or
- spanners for tightening bolts
- tape measure
- spirit level
- handyman's knife for cutting roofing felt
- extra preservative
- interior fittings as required

CHECK
- that all components have been pressure-treated with wood preservative; some cheaper sheds simply have the treatment brushed on.

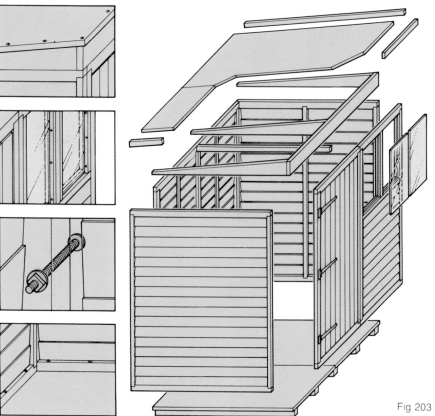

Fig 203

Fig 203 Prefabricated outbuildings such as sheds consist of four framed wall panels, a pitched or flat roof (usually supplied in sections except for very small buildings) and a floor. Start the assembly by setting the floor section(s) on a firm, flat, dry base. Stand two adjacent wall panels on the edge of the floor and fix them together with bolts, screws or nails. Add the remaining wall sections, check that they are square and secure each one to the floor. Next, place the roof panels in position. Finish the building off by adding the roofing felt, glazing the window(s) and hanging the door.

Putting up a Shed

Now add the other walls in the same way, checking that each is carefully aligned with the floor edge. When the shell is complete, nail or screw through the bottom rails of each wall panel into the floor itself to lock the walls in place.

Finish the construction by lifting the roof panels into place; pent roofs usually have a one-piece roof panel, while ridged roofs have two. Fix them down with nails, screws or, best of all, fixing brackets, and then add the roofing felt, turning it with edge battens. Finally, glaze the windows (using putty, even if this was not supplied with the kit) and give the exterior an extra coat of wood preservative.

If you plan to use your outbuilding as a workshop or for hobby activities, it is a good idea to insulate the walls by fitting slabs of rigid polystyrene between the frame battens and then covering them with tempered (damp-resistant) hardboard. You can add floor insulation too, covered with chipboard. Fix shelves and other internal fittings directly to the walls' framing battens.

Fig 204 (*above*) Garden sheds and other prefabricated outbuildings come in a wide range of shapes, sizes and styles.

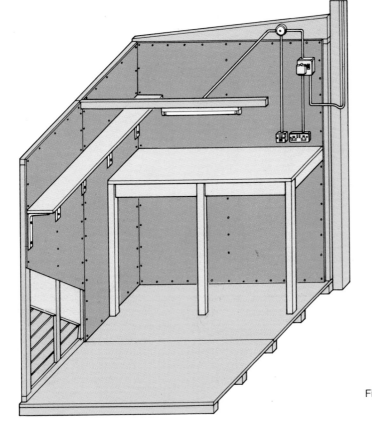

Fig 205

Fig 205 If you plan to use your shed as a workshop or hobbies room, fix rigid polystyrene foam insulation boards to the walls and then line them with tempered mositure-resistant hardboard. Fix shelf brackets direct to the wall framing, and build in a workbench with sturdy legs. Bring in a power supply so you have light and can plug in power tools and a heater.

Building a Porch

A well-designed porch is not just an attractive addition to your house; it has practical advantages too. It will protect a vulnerable front door from wind and rain, cutting down draughts and reducing heat losses. It is a useful place to dump things like wet shoes, and it improves home security and protecting doorstep callers.

The first stage in adding a porch to your home is the planning. You have to decide where it is going to be built, how big it will be, and what style you like. Site and size will generally be dictated by the layout of your house. A porch at the front may be a three-sided affair, or may extend across from an existing bay window. If you already have a recessed front door, you may simply have to add an infill panel to create an enclosed porch. Watch out for major obstructions on the house walls, such as soil pipes and downpipes, which may need rerouting.

The structure must sit on a firm, level base proofed against rising damp, and must also be weatherproofed where its walls and roof meet the house walls.

What to do

Start by removing any existing features like canopies, steps and downpipes that will not be incorporated in the new structure. Then mark out the floor area of the porch, and lay a concrete foundation slab 100mm (4in) thick over a base of well-rammed hardcore. If the slab will cover an existing air-brick in the house wall, incorporate a 100mm (4in) diameter duct of PVC pipe running to a new air-brick at the front of the slab. Brush on two coats of bitumen damp-proofer when the concrete has hardened to act as a damp-proof membrane. Do not forget to damp-proof the section of house wall that will be covered by the base. Next, bed courses of brickwork on the damp-proofed slab to form the outline of the porch base, and infill with a fine concrete screed, trowelled to a smooth finish.

Set the first frame in position over a strip of damp-course material. Secure the sill with rust-proof screws driven down into wallplugs in the brickwork beneath,

What you need:
- window frames
- door frame and door plus hinges and door furniture
- timber for roof structure, corner posts etc.
- roofing materials
- flashing strips
- exterior mastic
- DPC materials
- hard-core, bricks, mortar and concrete plus damp-proof membrane for base
- screws and wallplugs
- oval wire nails
- glass and putty
- building and woodworking tools

CHECK
- whether you need planning permission. Porches do not need permission so long as they have a floor area of no more than 3sq m (35sq ft), are not more than 3m (10ft) high and are at least 2m (6ft 6in) from the road. Porches are exempt from all Building Regualtions control.

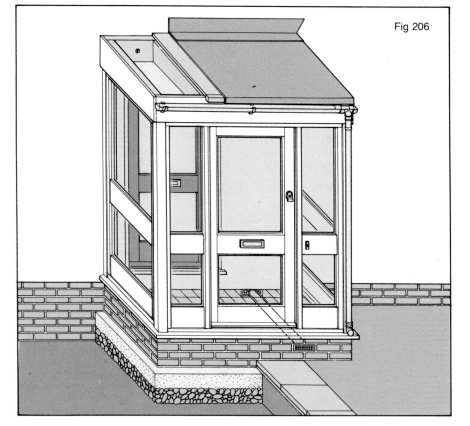

Fig 206

Fig 206 A typical build-out porch can be constructed using off-the-shelf window and door frames, linked together with corner posts to form a three-sided enclosure set on a dwarf wall that forms the porch base. The base should incorporate a damp-proof membrane linked to the damp course in the house wall, topped with a fine concrete screed to form the floor. Care must be taken not to block off any airbricks in the house wall by running ducting through the base to the outside air. The roof can be flat or pitched; the former is simpler to construct, and is topped with roofing felt sealed to the house wall with flashing.

and add the other frames in sequence, screwing them to each other and to the corner posts at the front of the porch. In addition, screw the frames to wallplugs set in the masonry where they meet the house walls. That completes the walls.

Next, attach a horizontal wallplate to the house wall with screws and wallplugs, about 25mm (1in) higher than the top front rail of the porch to give the roof a slight slope. Add joists between the wallplate and the front frame.

Cut a piece of 12mm (½in) exterior-grade plywood to size to form the roof decking, and screw it to the wallplate and porch framework. Cover it with a layer of heavy-duty roofing felt, fixed in place with clout nails, and turn the edges neatly down over the framework at the front and sides. Add timber fascias to hide the edge of the felt, and finish off the roof by sealing the join between it and the house wall with flashing strip.

Finish the job off by fitting the glass and sealing the join between the porch and the house wall with flexible mastic.

Fig 210

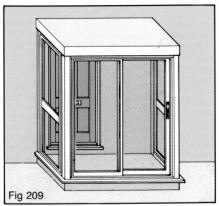

Fig 208

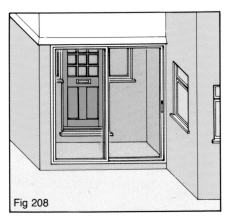

Fig 209

Fig 207 (*above*) A porch is a useful addition to any house, improving security and comfort.

Fig 208 Make use of adjoining walls where appropriate when constructing your porch.

Fig 209 You can include sliding patio doors in place of a conventional door, especially if the porch is too shallow for a hinged door to open into it.

Fig 210 If an external porch cannot be built – for example, where the door opens straight onto the pavement – it may be possible to construct a lobby within the house instead.

Putting up Fences

Unless you are fortunate enough to have a hedge or a wall around your property, you have little choice but to fence your boundaries — for privacy, for security, and to keep children and pets from straying. There is a wide range of fencing materials available, ranging from cheap wire mesh to more expensive solid timber and plastic fencing, but there is little doubt that timber is the favourite choice because of its combination of relative durability and comparative good looks.

The most usual ways of putting up timber fences involve either fixing prefabricated panels between the posts, or the more traditional nailing of boards to horizontal rails, known as weatherboarding. Fence panels come in several styles and sizes, usually made with horizontal strips of wood reinforced with battens. The strips may simply overlap each other, or may be interwoven round the battens. Weatherboarding consists of a series of individual tapered boards (known as feather-edge boards) fixed vertically to the support rails so each one overlaps its neighbours.

What to do

Whichever type of fencing you decide to put up, success or failure depends on the care with which you erect the fence posts. The best way of securing a post is to bury one quarter of its length in the ground, with a collar of concrete round it to hold it securely. An alternative which is quicker to use in firm ground is the metal fence spike, which is driven into the ground with a sledge-hammer and has a socket into which the fence post is secured.

Start by marking out the line of the fence along the boundary so you can decide where to place the posts. If you are using panel fencing these must be precisely positioned to allow the panels (which are usually 2m (6ft 6in) wide) to fit neatly between them. The end panel of a run of fencing may have to be cut down in width. With weatherboard fences, post spacing is less critical since the rails can be cut to length to match the post spacing once they have been set in position.

With panel fencing, erect the first post

What you need:
- posts plus concrete or fence spikes
- scrap timber and nails for bracing posts
- tape measure
- string lines
- spirit level
- gravel boards
- post caps
- galvanized nails
- claw hammer

For panel fences:
- fence panels
- panel clips

For boarded fences:
- arris rails plus brackets
- fence boards

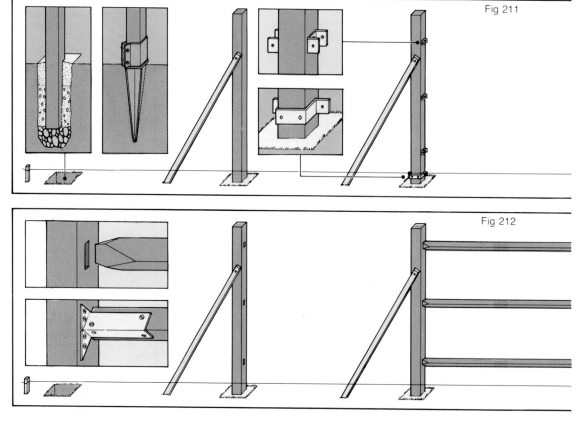

Fig 211

Fig 212

and brace it upright with scrap timber. Then offer up a panel, mark the post postion, set it in place and fit the first panel while the concrete is still wet so you can make any adjustments necessary to get a good fit. Brace the second post as before, and carry on along the run adding panels and posts in turn. At the end of the run, measure the panel width required, prise off the edge battens at one side of the panel and cut through the strips. Then replace the battens along the edge of the cut-down panel and fit it in place.

With weatherboarding, set the whole line of posts in place, braced upright as before, and leave for 24 hours for the concrete to harden. Then cut and fit the arris rails — two for fences up to 1.2m (4ft) high, three for higher fences — and start nailing on the boards. Fit the first with its thicker edge tight against the post, then add subsequent boards so each overlaps its neighbouring board by about 12mm (½in). Use a spirit level to check that each board is upright, and complete the run with the last board reversed.

Fig 213 (*above*) Timber fencing comes in a range of styles and is easy to erect on any site.

Fig 211 With panel fencing, the posts must be set at spacings that match the panels' width to ensure that they fit. Set the posts in concrete or use fence spikes, then fit the brackets in place with fence clips. Add gravel boards and fence caps to complete the job.

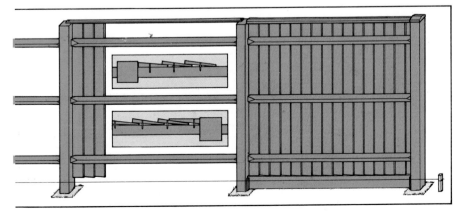

Fig 212 With post-and-rail fencing post spacing is not so critical; you can always cut the rails to length if necessary. Either fit them in mortises cut in the posts or use arris rail brackets to secure them. Then nail on the boards one by one, overlapping them slightly and checking that they are vertical as you work along the rails. Reverse the last board against the post.

Hanging a Gate

If you want to discourage people (not to mention animals) from straying onto your property from the street, the best solution – whether you have a fence, a wall or a hedge along the frontage – is to put up a gate. For pedestrian access you need nothing more substantial than a timber or metal gate about 1m (3ft 3in) wide, set between a pair of timber posts, and this is a simple enough job to carry out. Wider gates allowing vehicle access are another matter; because of their much greater weight, they need really substantial support – ideally in the form of a masonry pier at the hinge side, although large timber posts can be used so long as they are adequately set in sturdy concrete footings. You may prefer to leave their installation to a builder.

For a small gate leading to a path, buy or make the gate first so you can then set the post spacing to match. Use 75mm (3in) square preservative-treated fence posts for gates up to 1m (3ft) high, and 100mm (4in) posts for higher gates. Allow for one quarter of the post length to buried.

What to do

Start by cutting the posts to length, and cut the tops at an angle so they will shed water unless you plan to fit post caps. Then use scrap timber to make up a jig that will hold the posts parallel to each other and far enough apart to allow the gate to fit between them with clearance for the hinge knuckles at one side and the catch at the other.

Dig the post holes and set the assembled jig in place, using braces of scrap timber to hold it upright. Stand each post on some hard-core to prevent it from becoming waterlogged, and tamp in a concrete collar round each one. Check with a spirit level that the jig is upright, and leave the concrete to harden for 24 hours.

Next, remove the jig timber and set the gate in position between the posts, with packing pieces beneath it to ensure that it will clear the path surface when the gate is opened. Drive nails into the post faces to hold it temporarily in place while you attach the hinges and catch.

What you need:
- new gate
- hinges and catch
- fixing screws
- gate posts
- scrap timber and nails for post jig and for bracing posts
- tape measure
- claw hammer
- concrete for setting posts
- spirit level
- bradawl
- screwdriver

CHECK
- that the posts are set truly vertical.
- that there is sufficient clearance beneath the gate for it to open if the path slopes.
- that you fit a closing spring to shut the gate automatically if you have pets or small children.

Fig 214

Fig 215

Fig 216

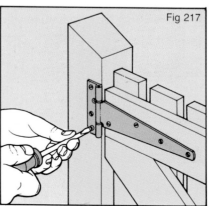

Fig 217

Fig 214 Use scrap timber to make up a jig that will hold the gate posts the correct distance apart.

Fig 215 Dig the post holes and set the assembled jig in place with concrete. Check that it is vertical, then brace it until the concrete has hardened.

Fig 216 Remove the jig timbers and set the gate in place on spacers to ensure it will clear the path surface as it opens and closes.

Fig 217 Use nails to hold the gate between the posts while you fit the hinges and catch.

REPAIR JOBS

With so much wood used in the construction and fitting-out of the average house, it is hardly surprising that you are likely to have to carry out maintenance and repair jobs at fairly regular intervals to keep everything in good working order. Wood is a surprisingly tough and resilient material, but can suffer if it is neglected (especially out of doors) or maltreated.

Out of doors, rot is public enemy number one, and any softwood that is not protected from the weather by paint, varnish, stain or preservative will soon be attacked by wet rot. This will leave the wood in a weakened and spongy condition that also looks extremely unsightly.

Indoors, wear and tear take their toll of timber fittings. Windows and doors begin to bind in their frames, while floors and staircases can develop splits (not to mention creaks, which can be intensely annoying). Even furniture can suffer, with loose or warped joints affecting framed furniture, while cupboards and chest may have worn drawer runners or loose hinges.

A Woodwork Checklist

It is a good idea to give your house's woodwork a regular check-up to make sure that trouble is not brewing anywhere.

Outdoors, pay particular attention to the condition of wooden windows and doors. The likeliest places for rot to gain a foothold are along sills, where side frame members meet the sills, and along glazing bars where open joints can easily admit water. Test for rot by pushing a slim penknife blade into the wood; if it goes in easily by more than a few millimetres, be suspicious and investigate further by stripping off the decorative finish to establish the extent of the outbreak.

Check the condition of timber fence posts, panels and boards too, especially close to ground level. Rotten timber is weak timber, likely to found out by the next gale, and replacement is usually the only viable solution.

Indoors, check that windows and doors open and close smoothly. Watch out for paint build-up on edges that can cause binding, and for sagging or loose hinges on doors and side-hung windows. Check

sash windows to make sure the cords and pulleys are working smoothly; you should replace any cords that are frayed or broken. Note any cracks in panes of glass.

Whenever you are lifting floor coverings during redecoration or for replacement, take the opportunity to check the condition of the underlying structure. Boards may be loose, split or even damaged by woodworm or rot. On staircases, treads may be loose or may have damaged nosings, and handrails may not be as secure as they should be.

Lastly, keep an eye on the condition of your furniture, so you can carry out simple repairs to areas of weakness or damage before they fail altogether.

Fig 218 (*above*) Many of the repairs every house needs from time to time involve trying to keep outdoor woodwork in good condition.

Fig 219 (*left*) If a window gets broken, prompt replacement is called for and the skill of a glazier is well worth acquiring. You can even take the opportunity to replace a broken pane with sealed-unit double glazing.

Filling and Patching Woodwork

An inspection of your woodwork is likely to reveal an assortment of minor blemishes and major faults. The minor blemishes will include dents and other signs of physical damage (mainly indoors), while the major faults are more likely to be out of doors and caused by wet rot attack. You should be able to patch up the former with little more than some carefully-applied wood filler, but in the case of the latter some more drastic repairs such as letting in new timber may be called for.

What to do

If you want to give your woodwork a top-quality finish, you will want to conceal any surface blemishes as far as possible. You can fill dents, splits and other small-scale damage in wood that will be painted or varnished by using an appropriate proprietary wood filler (matching the wood colour if the piece is to be varnished). It is better to avoid the use of cellulose-type fillers, because these set hard and so can tend to crack and fall out as the wood expands and contracts with temperature and humidity changes. Fillers work best if they are applied to bare wood, so if you are preparing wood with an existing finish for redecoration, strip the finish from the area of the blemish before filling it. Apply the filler with a flexible filling knife, working it in across the grain first and then along the grain. Aim to leave the filling slightly proud of the surrounding wood so you can sand it down perfectly flush when it has hardened.

You can use special exterior-quality fillers in a similar way to patch up small areas of rot affecting outdoor woodwork. However, you must first of all chisel out any wood that has been seriously damaged; then brush on a special resin hardening agent before filling the damaged area with the filler. To keep further rot attacks at bay, drill holes into sound wood round the repaired areas and insert special pellets of solid preservative into the holes, covering them with filler. Any moisture that penetrates the wood will dissolve the pellets and release the preservative.

If rot has caused serious damage to outdoor woodwork such as door and window frames, the scale of the repair will generally be too great for filler to be used satisfactorily, and you will have little option

Fig 220 (*above*) Treat bare wood with preservative before repainting, to help keep rot at bay.

Fig 221

Fig 222

Fig 221 Tackle small areas of rot or other damage by pressing exterior-quality filler into the damaged area. Leave the filler standing slightly proud of the surrounding wood surface.

Fig 222 When the filler has hardened, sand it down flush with the surrounding wood surface, and paint to protect it from the elements.

Filling and Patching Woodwork

but to cut out the affected area and to let in a piece of new wood to replace it. At the foot of a door frame, for example, rot can easily affect the wood from the sill upwards, and it also attacks window sills in a similar way.

Use a penknife to probe the wood and establish the size of the affected area. Then cut out the rot, making angled cuts if possible to increase the contact area be-tween the patch and the existing wood, and lever or chisel the damaged section away. If possible, use it as a pattern to mark up the replacement patch, matching the angles of the cut ends carefully. Then glue and screw the patch into place, and use filler to conceal the joint line if the patch is a less-than-perfect fit.

Always treat any patches generously with preservative before fitting them.

What you need:
- exterior-quality filler
- filling knife
- abrasive paper
- sanding block
- tenon or panel saw
- crowbar
- replacement timber
- pencil *or* marking knife
- power drill plus twist and masonry bits
- screwdriver
- screws and wallplugs
- woodworking adhesive
- cramps (improvised)
- plane

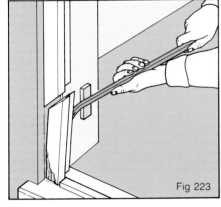

Fig 223

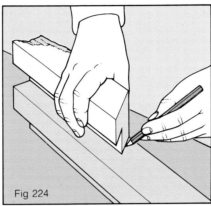

Fig 224

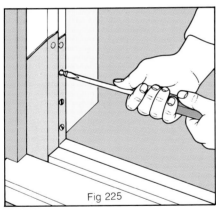

Fig 225

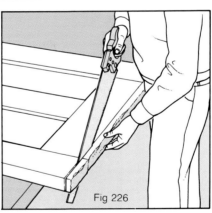

Fig 226

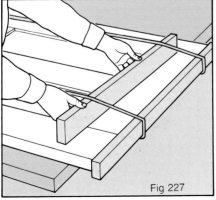

Fig 227

Fig 228

Fig 223 Where rot has affected the lower section of a door frame, make an angled saw cut through it just above the rotten section and lever this away with a crowbar.

Fig 224 Use the cut-out portion to mark up some fresh timber, and cut the patch to size.

Fig 225 Check the patch for fit, then glue and screw it into place. Countersink and fill the screw holes for an almost invisible repair.

Fig 226 If rot has also affected the foot of the door itself, take it off its hinges and saw off the rotten section.

Fig 227 Cut a strip of preservative-treated timber the same thickness as the offcut but slightly wider, and glue and screw it to the bottom of the door. Improvise some way of cramping it while the adhesive sets.

Fig 228 Then plane the strip down until it precisely matches the door thickness.

Repairing Wooden Windows

One of the commonest problems with casement windows is that of the opening casement or top light binding in its frame. This can be more than a nuisance, since forcing the jammed window open or slamming it shut can crack or break the glass. There are several causes; paint build-up over the years, moisture penetration causing the wood to swell in wet weather, hinges sagging, or joints opening up and causing the window to hang out of square.

Rot is the other major enemy for all wooden windows, and especially for casements with their exposed joints. As wooden windows are traditionally given a paint finish, rot can attack unnoticed, leading to eventual joint failure.

You may also have trouble with the window fittings — fixing screws pulling out of the wood, hinges rusting and so on.

With sash windows, similar problems of binding and joint failure can affect the sliding sashes, and rot can affect both sashes and frame, but it is breaks in the cords operating the sashes that generally cause the most frequent problems.

What to do: Casements

When a casement or top light is hard to open or close, do not force it if it is stuck closed, since the last thing you want to do is crack or break the glass. Instead, free it by tapping the stile opposite the hinges using a hammer and a softwood offcut to protect the wood.

If excessive paint build-up is to blame, strip both casement and rebate back to bare wood and then apply fresh primer, undercoat and topcoat. If necessary, plane a little wood off the outer edge of the casement to increase the clearance first.

The binding may be caused by the casement itself being out of square, and this is often due to the corner joints opening up. The simplest way of squaring up a casement is to drive dowel pegs through the corner joints, or to attach L-shaped corner repair brackets to each corner of the frame. These can be surface-mounted, but you can make the repair less obtrusive by recessing them into the wood and disguising their presence with filler.

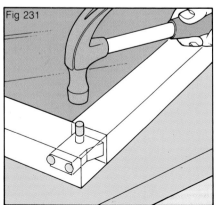

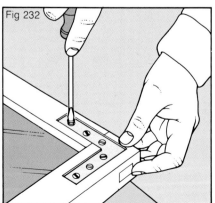

What you need:
- plane or Surform
- primer, undercoat and topcoat or microporous paint
- paintbrush
- power drill and dowel bit
- fluted dowels
- woodworking adhesive
- hammer
- metal repair plates
- chisel
- bradawl
- screwdriver
- woodscrews

For sash windows:
- chisel
- handyman's knife
- pincers
- new sash cord
- string
- clout nails
- hammer

CHECK
- that you do not crack the glass as you try to square up a distorted casement or sash.

Fig 229 If casement windows are binding in their frames, strip excess paint from the closing edge and plane off a little extra wood.

Fig 230 Then prime, undercoat and top-coat the bare wood.

Fig 231 If corner joints are opening up and causing the frame to sag, you may be able to strengthen the joint by drilling holes through it and driving in lengths of glued dowel.

Fig 232 An alternative is to cut shallow recesses in the wood so you can screw on metal repair plates. Cover the repair with filler.

Repairing Wooden Windows

What to do: Sliding Sashes

Old-fashioned sash windows operated by weights and cords that are concealed in the side frames of the window suffer from one major problem: broken sash cords, leaving the upper sash refusing to stay closed and the lower one refusing to remain open. The big drawback with this type of window is that repairing the sashes means prising off the beadings that form the channels in which the sashes slide, then removing the sash concerned so access can be gained to weights in their hidden pockets at each side of the frame. You can then remove the old cords, thread in new ones (made from unbreakable polypropylene cord to avoid the need for future replacement), attach one end to the weight and nail the other back to the side of the sash. Reverse the procedure to reassemble the window.

If your sash windows rattle in high winds, you may be able to improve things by slightly repositioning the beads. Adding draught-proofing helps too.

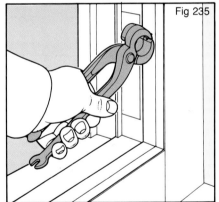

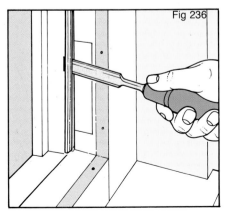

Fig 233 (*above*) You generally have to strip paint from windows before you can assess what repairs are needed. Take care not to crack the glass when using a blowlamp or hot-air gun.

Fig 234 To remove the sashes, start by gently levering the staff bead away from the frame.

Fig 235 Then use pliers or pincers to prise out the fixing pins so you can remove the bead without damaging it.

Fig 236 Lift the inner sash away from the frame so a helper can cut through the sash cords at each side of the window. Then prise off the parting bead.

Fig 237 Now repeat the lifting and cord-cutting to remove the outer sash from the frame.

73

Replacing Sash Cords

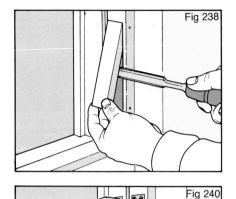

Fig 238

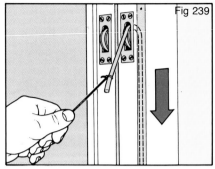

Fig 239

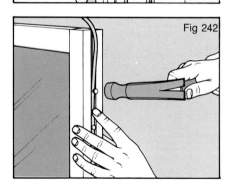

Fig 240

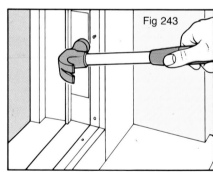

Fig 241

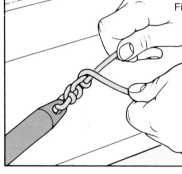

Fig 242

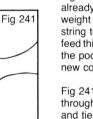

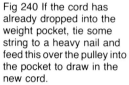

Fig 243

Fig 238 Prise off the covers of the pockets at each side of the frame to get at the weights.

Fig 239 If the cord is still over the pulley, tie some string to it and draw the old cord out so the string is pulled through and can be used to draw in the new sash cord.

Fig 240 If the cord has already dropped into the weight pocket, tie some string to a heavy nail and feed this over the pulley into the pocket to draw in the new cord.

Fig 241 Pull the cord out through the pocket opening and tie it to the weight.

Fig 242 Nail the other ends of the two cords temporarily to the sides of the sash, securing each with a single nail, about 100mm (4in) below the top of the sash.

Fig 243 After adjusting the cord position (see Fig 244), replace the pocket covers and beads.

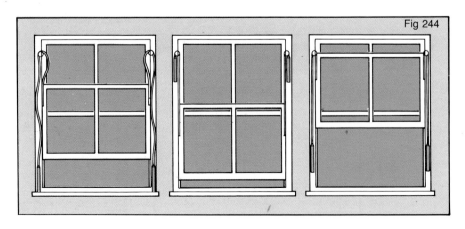

Fig 244

Fig 244 (From right to left) Hold the sash in its channel and allow the weights to operate it. If it will not go right up, move the top nail fixing the cord to the sash down a little. If it will not go right down, move the cord up the edge of the sash slightly and re-nail it. If the weights hit the bottom of the pockets before the sash is fully open, move the cord down the edge of the sash to shorten it.

Glazing a Window

A broken window is one of those jobs you need to attend to immediately if your home is to remain weatherproof and secure. It is always a good idea to keep some heavy-duty polythene sheeting to hand so you can make a temporary repair.

What to do

If the glass is just cracked, reinforce it temporarily with adhesive tape. However, if it is shattered you should immediately lift out all the pieces for safety. Wear stout gloves, and make sure you dispose of the debris safely. Then use an old chisel or similar tool to hack out the old putty.

Next, measure up for the glass, subtracting 3mm (⅛in) from each dimension for clearance, and order a replacement pane plus some putty. Press a thin layer of bedding putty into the rebate, bed the glass in place and secure it with sprigs. Then add the facing putty, finish it off to a neat 45° bevel with a putty knife and trim the bedding putty indoors. Paint within fourteen days.

Fig 245 (*above*) If a window gets broken, prompt replacement is called for. You can take this opportunity to replace a broken pane with sealed-unit double glazing.

Fig 246

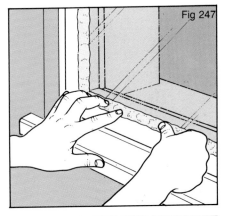

Fig 247

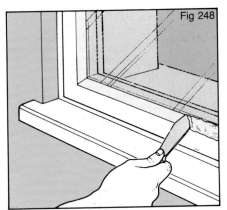

Fig 248

Fig 249

Fig 246 Carefully lift out the broken pieces of glass with gloved hands, then hack away all the old putty.

Fig 247 Put new bedding putty all round, press the new pane into it and secure it with glazing sprigs. Then add the facing putty all round the pane.

Fig 248 Finish off the facing putty neatly with a putty knife.

Fig 249 Finally trim off any excess bedding putty indoors.

Curing Door Faults

Doors, especially interior ones, get more wear and tear than almost any other component of the house. They are each opened and closed dozens of times a day, and any weakness in their hinges or latches will soon show up as a result. Loose or damaged hinges will cause the door to sag and will either prevent it from closing properly or make it difficult to open. This in turn imposes strain on the door furniture, with handles pulling away from the door a common result as you attempt to wrench it open. It also moves latches out of alignment, again resulting in sticking and premature wear and damage.

Another common problem is that of doors binding along their bottom edges as a result of new, thicker floor coverings being laid. Here the remedy is quite straightforward; to saw or plane some wood off the bottom edge of the door so it will clear the new floor level comfortably. If you are laying thick floor covering materials such as ceramic or quarry tiles, it is vital to shorten the door *before* laying new floor if you are not to be trapped!

What to do

If a door is binding in its frame, try to establish first of all what the cause is. It may be nothing more troublesome than a build-up of paint on the door edge and within the door rebate as a result of repeated redecoration, and if this is the case it is a simple job to use abrasive paper or a tool such as a Surform plane to remove a little of the paint. This may cure a case of mild binding, but if it does not you will have to strip the paint back to bare wood, ready for repainting, and perhaps remove a few extra shavings of wood from the door edge as well.

You can use a similar technique to cure slight binding of the door on its threshold, by moving it repeatedly to and fro over a pad of abrasive material placed beneath the door edge.

Next, check that the screws securing the hinges to the door and its frame are secure. Remove any that are loose, and either replace them with slightly longer screws of the same gauge or push glued

What you need:
- abrasive paper
- sanding block
- plane or rasp
- touch-up paint
- wedges
- longer screws
- screwdriver
- pencil
- board offcut
- matchsticks *or* fluted dowels
- power drill plus twist drill bit
- woodworking adhesive

TIP
If hinge screw heads are filled with paint, chip this out before trying to loosen them. If the screws still will not shift, try angling the screwdriver tip in the screw slot so you can tap it with a hammer in an anti-clockwise direction. Next, try applying heat to the screw with a soldering iron. If all else fails, drill off the screw head to release the hinge.

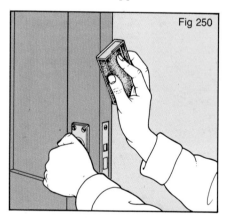

Fig 250 Ease sticking points on door edges with glasspaper wrapped round a sanding block.

Fig 251 Do the same for door bottoms by moving the door backwards and forwards over a pad of abrasive paper.

Fig 252 If the door seems to be sagging, wedge it upright so you can tighten the hinge fixing screws.

Curing Door Faults

matchsticks into the screwholes before replacing the original screws. Where the screwholes are badly damaged, it is better to remove the hinge completely, drill out the holes, glue in lengths of dowel and then make new pilot and clearance holes for the hinge screws.

Make sure that screw heads are properly seated flush within the hinge countersinks. Replace any that are standing proud with screws of a smaller gauge.

Where doors are fitted with rising butt hinges (*see* page 47), you may need to bevel off the top edge of the door slightly at the hinge side to allow it to clear the door frame as it opens and closes. Use a plane or rasp for this.

If you need to shorten a door to clear a new floor covering, use a specimen laid against the bottom of the door to see how much needs removing. Mark a line across the face of the door, then remove it from its frame so you can plane or saw off the excess wood. Leave rehanging the door until the new floor covering has been laid in case further adjustments are needed.

Fig 253 (*above*) You can often stop a door from rattling by slightly repositioning the keeper on the door frame.

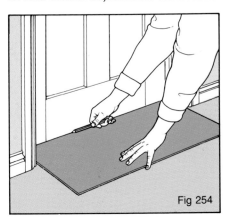

Fig 254

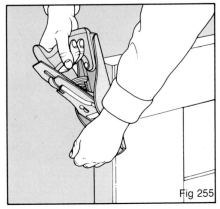

Fig 255

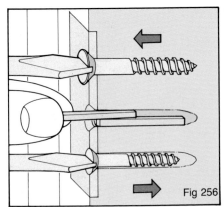

Fig 256

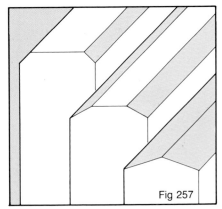

Fig 257

Fig 254 If you need to shorten a door so it will clear new, thicker floor coverings, use a board offcut to mark the cutting line on the foot of the door face.

Fig 255 Remove the door from its hinges and plane or saw off the excess wood down to the marked line.

Fig 256 If hinge screws are loose, unscrew them one at a time and push glued matchsticks into the screw holes. Then replace the screws.

Fig 257 A door hung on rising butt hinges may catch the top of the frame as it opens. The solution is to bevel the top edge of the door.

Repairing Timber Floors

In a traditionally built house, the floors are the biggest wooden component of all apart from the roof structure. The faults that floors suffer from fall into two main categories: superficial and serious. Superficial faults include such problems as shrinkage which causes gaps to open up between boards; splits caused by careless lifting of boards for access to services in the floor voids; surface damage – dents, stains, burn marks and so on – and general surface deterioration. Most can be put right relatively easily.

Serious faults include rot, (especially dry rot which can lead to complete collapse of the floor structure), woodworm attack, and sagging due to overloading of an inadequate structure or subsidence of the supporting brickwork. Rot attacks are usually confined to ground floors, although they can affect upstairs floors too if structural or plumbing faults result in wood remaining damp for any length of time. Serious woodworm attacks may cause structural weakness, although most merely mar the floor's appearance.

What to do

If your inspection reveals boards that are loose – perhaps because the wood has warped, or because boards have been lifted and not properly secured again – it is better to use screws rather than nails to fix them down. Warped boards will pull new nails up again, while a screw will hold the warped edge or end down securely; boards that have been lifted once may need lifting again and a screw is easier to remove than a nail. Check that all nail heads are punched in just below the surface of the boards.

If you find boards that have been split by careless lifting or over-loading, prise up the damaged board after cutting through the tongues along each edge. Use a jig saw to make transverse cuts over a joist line to cut out a section smaller than a complete board. Repair the split with woodworking adhesive, and secure the board back in place with nails or screws driven through new pilot holes so you do not cause fresh splits in the wood.

What you need:
- tenon, floorboard, jig or circular saw
- bolster and hammer
- scrap timber
- power drill plus twist drill bit
- screws
- screwdriver
- nails
- hammer
- new floorboard(s)
- folding wedges *or* floorboard cramps

CHECK
- the whereabouts of underfloor pipes and cables when sawing through the tongues or ends of floorboards. Boards that have obviously been lifted before are especially suspect.

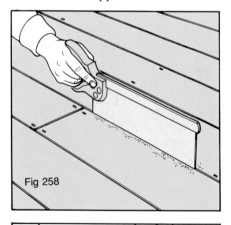

Fig 258

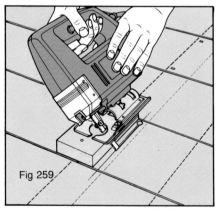

Fig 259

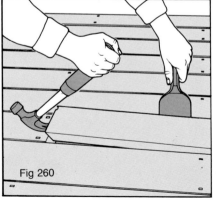

Fig 260

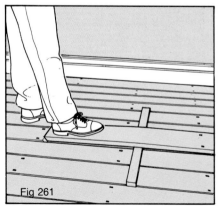

Fig 261

Fig 258 To lift a tongue-and-groove floorboard, first saw through the tongues at each side of the board.

Fig 259 If you do not want to lift the whole board, cut across it at an angle next to the joist line using a jig saw or pad saw. Use a block of wood to reduce the depth of cut in case there are cables just beneath the board.

Fig 260 Use a bolster and claw hammer to prise up one end of the board.

Fig 261 You can 'spring' long boards free from their nails by laying a batten beneath the lifted end and then treading down on it.

Repairing Timber Floors

Lastly, check for gaps between boards which will admit draughts and dust. If you intend to lay fitted floor coverings, it is not worth trying to fill them; simply nail down a thin hardboard or plywood overlay to stop the draughts and provide a firm, flat surface. However, if you intend to leave the boards on show, the gaps will have to be dealt with, and the only real cure-all is to lift and re-lay the boards with the gaps between them closed up.

If you plan to re-lay the boards, you need some form of cramp to drive the boards tightly together. You can use an old broad-bladed chisel dug into the top edge of each joist as a lever to wedge each board up against its neighbour. Alternatively, lay groups of four or five boards and then cramp them tightly together before nailing them down, using either folding timber wedges or a special floorboard cramp (available from plant hire shops). Once you have re-laid all the existing boards you will be left with a gap at one side of the room, which you will have to fill with a new board.

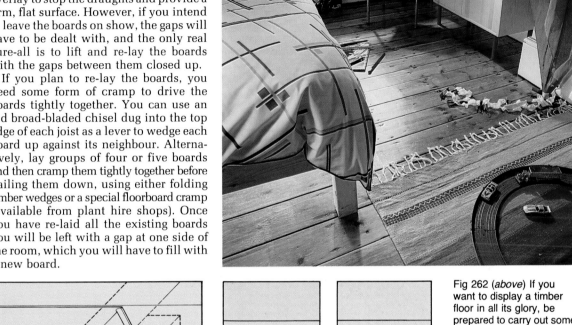

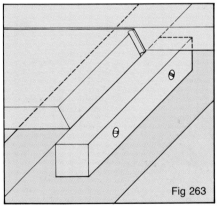

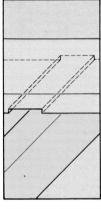

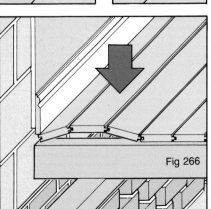

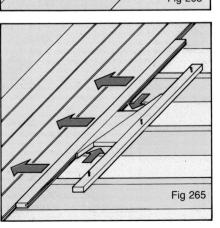

Fig 262 (*above*) If you want to display a timber floor in all its glory, be prepared to carry out some localized repairs.

Fig 263 Fix a short batten to the side of the joist to support the end of the replacement board.

Fig 264 If the replacement board is thicker than its neighbours, cut a shallow recess in its underside to fit over the joist. Fix packing if it is thinner.

Fig 265 Use folding wedges as shown to cramp re-laid boards tightly together.

Fig 266 At the edge of the room, spring the last three boards into place in one operation after slotting them together loosely.

Repairing Staircases

A timber staircase consists of a series of evenly-spaced horizontal treads which form the flight. Most staircases also have vertical risers which fill the space between the rear edge of one tread and the front edge of the tread above; these may be nailed in place, or may have tongued edges which slot into grooves in the front and back edges of the treads.

The treads are supported at each side by two parallel timbers called strings. A closed-string staircase has the treads and risers set into grooves cut in the inner faces of the strings, while an open-string staircase has the outer string cut in a zig-zag fashion so the treads can rest on the cut-outs. The inner string – the one against the wall of the stairwell – is always a closed string. On wide stairs the treads may receive additional support from a length of timber called a carriage, set beneath the centre line of the flight.

Such a complex construction can expect to suffer its fair share of everday problems, but some of these at least are fairly simple to cure.

What to do

The commonest problem with stairs are creaks caused if one of the components has become loose. A cure is simple if the underside of the flight is accessible, but less straightforward if it is not.

If you can gain access to the underside of the flight, the best way of curing the problem is to screw and glue blocks of wood into the internal angles between the treads and risers. Check that the screws you use are not overlong, or they may break through the face of the tread or riser above; the risers may be of thinner timber then the treads.

If the creak still persists, check the external angle where the back edge of the tread meets the bottom edge of the riser. To correct any movement here, drive screws through one component into the other.

While you are underneath the staircase, check whether the timber wedges holding the treads and risers in their slots in the strings are secure, and tap any that are loose back into place.

What you need:
- hammer
- woodworking adhesive
- reinforcing blocks
- power drill plus twist drill bit
- screws
- screwdriver
- metal angle brackets
- chisel
- jigsaw plus fence attachment
- replacement timber
- plane or rasp

TIP
If you have to expose the underside of a boxed-in staircase, take the opportunity to check for traces of woodworm or dry rot, and get professional advice if you find evidence of an attack.

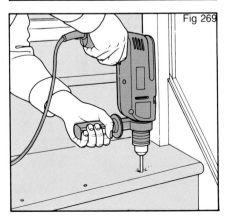

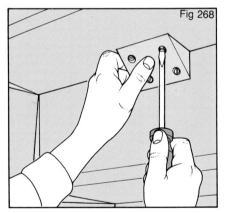

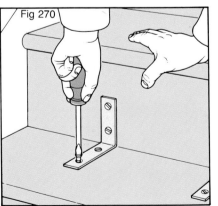

Fig 267 If you can gain access to the underside of the flight, tackle creaking treads by tapping the fixing wedges firmly back into their slots in the staircase strings at each side.

Fig 268 Glue and screw reinforcing blocks into the angles between treads and risers. Check that the screws do not pass right through the woodwork.

Fig 268 If you cannot gain access to the underside of the flight, drill holes so you can drive screws down through the treads into the risers below.

Fig 270 Add L-shaped repair brackets in the angle between treads and risers. They will be concealed by the stair carpet.

Repairing Staircases

If your staircase is plastered underneath, you will have to remove the stair carpet to get at the joints between the fronts of the treads and the tops of the risers first. Prise each one apart with a chisel if you can, and run a bead of woodworking adhesive along the joint. Then drill two or three evenly-spaced clearance holes in each tread, in line with the centre of the riser below, and drive in 38mm (1½in) screws to pull the two components together. At the internal angles between tread and riser, fit L-shaped metal repair brackets to pull the two components tightly together. Chisel out shallow recesses to make the brackets less noticeable.

Wear and tear or accidental damage can result in the nosing – the projecting front edge of an individual tread – becoming worn or split. Here the solution is to remove the damaged part of the tread and fit a new piece of wood in its place. Cut out the section carefully with a tenon saw and a jig saw, then cut a patch to fit and glue and screw it in place. Finally, plane it down to match its surroundings.

Fig 271 (*above*) Staircases are complex pieces of joinery, but seldom need major repairs.

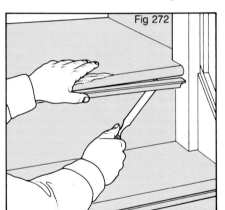

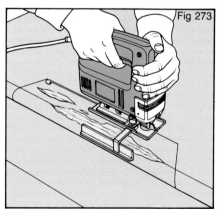

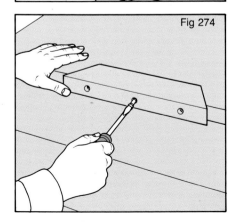

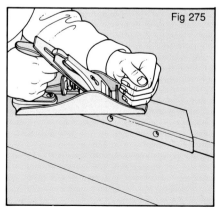

Fig 272 To repair a damaged tread nosing, first prise off any beading beneath the nosing.

Fig 273 Then mark out the area to be patched and cut along the grain with a jig-saw or pad saw. Make the angled cuts with a tenon saw.

Fig 274 Cut an over-sized patch and glue and screw it into place.

Fig 275 Plane the patch down to match the level of the surrounding wood.

Simple Furniture Repairs

Furniture of all sorts has to take quite a pounding in the average home, and sooner or later something needs mending. Some of the commonest problems occur with chairs, which tend to get used for all sorts of unorthodox purposes as well as for just sitting on, and with the moving parts such as doors and drawers on cupboards and sideboards, which can wear out or be damaged by regular use.

Whatever the repair you are planning to carry out, your starting point is the same – assessing the damage and deciding how best to tackle the job. The problem may be a simple matter of repairing a loose joint which has come apart but is otherwise sound, or a more complex one of mending broken frame members or replacing pieces that have gone missing altogether. At this stage, you need to decide how much dismantling will be needed to allow you to carry out the repair, what additional materials will be required and also whether you will need any tools you do not currently have in your tool-kit. Then you are ready to start work.

What to do

If your chairs have loose joints anywhere, or there is any sign of 'play' if the chair is rocked, the joints need repair. You may be able to pull a loose joint like this apart enough to squeeze in some woodworking adhesive, and then to push it back together and leave it to set. Otherwise, dismantle it completely so you can carry out a proper repair.

Start by labelling any parts that might get muddled up during reassembly – mainly rails and stretchers. Then turn the chair upside down, and remove any corner blocks underneath the seat.

You are now ready to knock the joints apart, and to do this you need a mallet or hammer and a block of scrap softwood. Once you have dismantled all the loose joints, carefully remove all traces of the old adhesive. With all the joints cleaned up, you can reverse the dismantling procedure and reassemble your chair. Make up either front and back or left and right side assemblies first, and then complete

What you need:
- mallet
- abrasive paper
- sanding block
- chisel
- woodworking adhesive
- sash cramps *or* tourniquet cramp
- reinforcing blocks
- power drill plus twist drill bits
- pencil
- scribing block
- tenon saw
- fluted dowels
- screwdriver

TIP
When trying to dismantle a piece of framed furniture which has loose joints, try to work out in which order the piece was originally assembled so you can dismantle the joints in the reverse order.

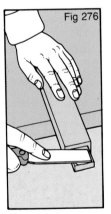
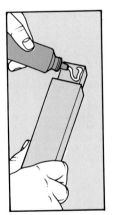

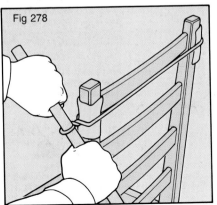
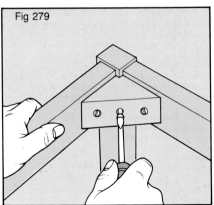

Fig 276 To repair a loose joint on framed furniture, start by prising the joint apart so you can remove any traces of old adhesive. Then spread on some fresh adhesive.

Fig 277 Reassemble the joint(s), using sash cramps if you have them to hold the joints tight while the adhesive sets.

Fig 278 Improvise cramps if necessary. A tourniquet can be very effective if used with packing to prevent damage to the wood surface.

Fig 279 Reinforce weak corner joints on chairs by gluing and screwing blocks inside the corners of the frame.

Simple Furniture Repairs

the assembly by linking these with rails and/or stretchers as required. Cramping is essential at each stage, using a portable workbench, a pair of sash cramps (which you can hire) or even a makeshift set of tourniquets.

Brush adhesive onto tenons and dowels, then reassemble the joints, applying the cramps with protective pads as soon as each assembly is complete. Do not overtighten the cramps, and check that the frames are square and untwisted before setting them aside for at least 24 hours to allow the glue to set properly. Wipe away any excess adhesive that oozes out of the joints before it has a chance to harden.

Drawers commonly suffer from loose joints and worn runners, while the commonest source of trouble with small doors is damage to the hinges, or more precisely to the wood surrounding their fixings, The door may have been forced or leant on, with the result that the wood has split around the screws. Both these problems are relatively simple to put right with a little ingenuity—see below.

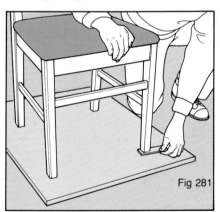

Fig 281

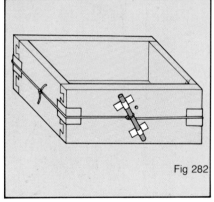

Fig 282

Fig 280 (*above*) Repair worn drawer runners by gluing strips of new wood to the bottom edges of the drawer sides and planing them down so they are perfectly smooth.

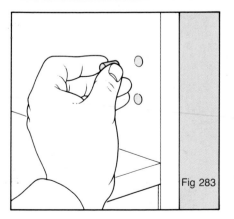

Fig 283

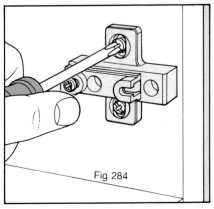

Fig 284

Fig 281 Level uneven legs by putting packing under the short leg until the piece is level. Use the packing as a guide for shortening the other legs.

Fig 282 Re-glue loose joints on drawers, and use a tourniquet cramp to hold them while the adhesive sets.

Fig 283 Drill out damaged hinge screw holes and glue in lengths of dowel.

Fig 284 The drill pilot holes and re-fix the hinge to the unit.

Boxing-In Services

There is one small woodworking job that is not quite a project and not really a repair: boxing in ugly pipework and other surface-mounted services such as power or aerial cables. It is a simple job to carry out, and worth doing because the resulting boxing looks much neater and tidier than what it is concealing.

What to do

Perhaps the ugliest pipe runs are vertical ones, running up walls to carry supply or heating pipework from one floor of the house to another. Plumbers usually try to run these in corners where possible, which makes boxing-in easier, but they may of necessity run down elsewhere. In either case, start by working out the dimensions of the boxing required and where the supporting battens will be positioned. Then fix these to the walls and screw on the cover strips. You can box in pipes running along skirting boards by fixing cover strips to a floor batten and to the top edge of the skirting board.

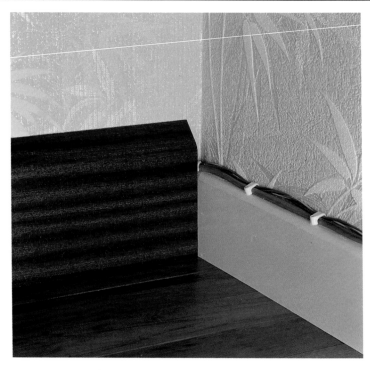

Fig 285 (*above*) You can box in cables and pipes and conceal old skirtings by fixing moulded cover strips over them.

What you need:
- battens/cover strips
- power drill plus twist and masonry bits
- screws and wallplugs
- screwdriver

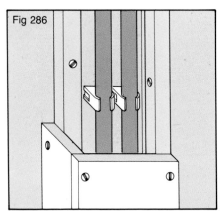

Fig 286

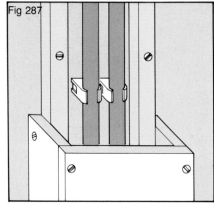

Fig 287

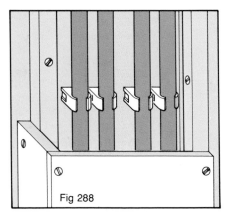

Fig 288

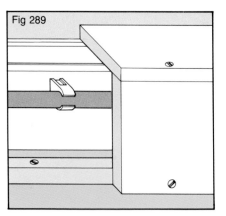

Fig 289

Fig 286 In corners, screw battens to the wall and add the two cover strips.

Fig 287 Make up U-shaped boxes to cover pipe runs in the middle of a wall.

Fig 288 Use plywood instead of solid timber as the facing for wider boxes concealing several pipes.

Fig 289 Hide pipe runs along skirtings with a front panel the same height as the skirting.

EXPENSIVE JOBS

However competent a do-it-yourselfer you are, there will be some jobs that are either too big for you to tackle or require professional skills and equipment. Examples include such major tasks as building a conservatory, converting a loft or putting in a new staircase, jobs which may not be beyond your skill if you are a very experienced woodworker, but which are likely to take too long if tackled on a DIY basis. In all these cases you may prefer to call in an outside contractor to do the work for you. This is a move that many people regard with some trepidation, since finding good, reliable tradesmen can be difficult and choosing the wrong firm could result not only in a bodged job but in considerable financial loss as well.

Here are some general guidelines to help you minimize the risk of picking a cowboy, followed by a look at what is involved in employing professionals.

Finding a Contractor

Once you have decided you need to call in a professional, your first step is to get people with the skills you require to visit the site and give you a firm quotation for the job.

Personal recommendation is by far the best and safest way of finding someone suitable. If a firm has already carried out work for friends, relatives or neighbours you will be able to get a first-hand account of its performance and even to check up on the standard of workmanship.

If this does not work, your next step is to take a walk or a drive round your area, looking for signs of someone carrying out the sort of work you want done. Many firms now put up a sign outside the site they are working on (or park their vans close by), and will not mind if you approach them. You can do this directly, or you can telephone the number on the sign or van. You can also approach householders directly if it is obvious that they have recently completed work similar to what you want doing. Most people are only too happy to show off a job well done and to put you in touch with the contractor concerned.

Next, you could try your telephone directories. Both list local contractors by trade, and many of the display advertisements not only give more details of the sort of work undertaken, but may also reveal whether the firm is a member of a relevant trade association. With this method, it is well worth asking the firm about other jobs it has done locally. Any company worth its salt will be pleased to put you in touch with satisfied customers.

Your last method of contact with local contractors is via the various professional and trade associations to which many reputable companies and individuals belong. These associations will give you the names and addresses of their members working in your area, and some offer other back-up services such as guarantees and arbitration schemes which may be worth knowing about. Membership of such a body is generally a good sign (many require evidence of several years' trading and satisfactory acounts before granting membership), but it is wise to check firms who claim membership with the body concerned — some firms simply 'borrow' logos and claim membership to enhance their image. For more details about individual woodworking and related trade associations, see page 94.

Fig 290 (*above*) Building a conservatory is a typical example of the larger scale job you may prefer to leave to a professional unless you can complete the project yourself within a reasonable time.

Getting Quotations

Once you have contacted someone who sounds interested in carrying out whatever work you want done, your next job is to explain clearly what the job involves and to find out as precisely as possible what it is going to cost you, when work can start and how long it will take to complete. For major projects such as building a conservatory or converting your loft it is essential not to rely on verbal agreements, but to ensure that everything is in writing. This can save a lot of argument, and will also help a court to sort a dispute out if things go seriously wrong. First, make sure that you understand the meaning of the following terms, so you know what you are asking for and what the contractor intends you to get.

- *Estimates* are just that – an educated guess as to the rough cost of the job. They are not legally binding.
- *Quotations* are firm offers to carry out a specified job for an agreed price. A quotation for a simple job should include details of material costs.
- *Tenders* are also offers to carry out specified work for a named price, but are understood to involve an element of competition with other contractors.

Most contractors will want to make a site visit to assess the scale of the job involved before even giving an estimate. Explain in as much detail as possible what you require, and tell him you must have a firm quotation for the work, plus details of when he will start and how long the job will take.

Ask at this point whether he or the firm is registered for VAT, and if so whether VAT is payable on the work you are having done. Generally speaking, you do not have to pay VAT on work involving the construction, alteration or demolition of a building, but VAT *is* payable on repair works and maintenance. If he is not a registered VAT trader (with a registration number printed on his notepaper), he cannot charge you VAT on work he does for you.

Always get at least two quotations for the job, and more if you can. This allows you to compare terms as well as prices before making your choice. Impossibly high quotes rarely mean you will get top-quality work; they are the contractor's way of saying he does not want the job, but will do it if you are prepared to pay a silly price.

Assessing Quotations

Once you have received the quotations, study them carefully. The amount of detail given will vary from firm to firm, but they should cover the following points:

- a description of the work to be carried out, preferably presented as a detailed list setting out all the stages involved.
- details of particular materials or fittings to be used for the project, and who will supply them.
- who will be responsible for obtaining any official permission needed.
- when the work will start.
- when the work will be completed.
- who will be responsible for insuring the work and materials on site.
- whether sub-contractors will be employed, and for which parts of the job.
- how variations to methods, timing or costs will be agreed.
- the total cost of the work.
- when payment will be required.

These details form part of the contract between you and whoever you decide to employ, so it is important that they are discussed and dealt with now, to prevent arguments later. Some firms may include them on a standard form of contract sent with the quotation, or may print their terms and conditions on the reverse of their quotation. In either case, read them carefully; now is the time to discuss any clauses you do not want to apply.

Once you have received quotations from the various firms you approached, it is up to you to decide which one to accept on the basis of price, timing and other factors such as your personal impressions or any recommendations you have received. When you have made your choice, write and accept the quotation . . . and notify unsuccessful applicants as a courtesy.

You now have a contract between yourself and the contractor. In most circumstances there is no reason to suppose that anything will go wrong but if it does, tackle it immediately so things can be put right. Mention problems verbally first of all, and if this does not resolve matters, follow up with a letter outlining the nature of your complaint and requesting specific action to correct it. Always keep notes of any discussions you have with the contractor, and copies of any letters you send, in case a dispute cannot be resolved and you have to go to independent arbitration.

FACTS AND FIGURES

This section is intended as a handy reference guide to the range of timber, man-made boards, woodworking fittings and sundry materials you will need to carry out the various jobs described earlier in the book. It will help you to see at a glance what is available, in what sizes or quantities, so you can plan your requirements in detail and draw up itemized shopping lists for individual projects.

Lastly, on page 94 there is a detailed glossary of all the terms used in the book, plus a list of useful addresses.

Natural Timber

Most wood in the home is softwood, a term that describes wood from coniferous or evergreen species such as pine, spruce, fir and larch – very much a utility wood. However, furniture and other fittings are more likely to be made from hardwood, which comes from deciduous trees – those that lose their leaves in autumn. This grouping includes many familiar temperate-zone species such as ash, beech, elm, oak and walnut, as well as a whole host of species that grow in the tropics – 'rain forest' trees such as mahogany, teak and sapele.

The list below gives you a guide to the commonest timber species, with details of its appearance, its properties, what it is commonly used for (and why), and what is the best way to finish it.

Beech This is a fine-textured European hardwood, ranging from pinkish (especially when steamed) to yellow-brown in colour and usually straight-grained. It often features tiny regular flecks of a darker colour. It bends easily, so is often used for bentwood furniture, and is also popular for kitchen worktops and utensils. It holds nails and tacks well, making it ideal for cabinet carcases and the frames of upholstered furniture. It is often left plain in kitchens, but otherwise may be finished with varnish.

Douglas fir This is one of the coniferous softwoods, more widely used for structural woodwork and internal joinery than for furniture, It has a reddish-brown colour

and a grain pattern that is quite pronounced and may be slightly wavy. It is almost free of knots, comes in wide boards and is easy to work. It is usually painted, but can be stained or varnished.

Hemlock This is another coniferous softwood, pale yellow (or even greyish) in colour and with a straight grain and moderately fine texture. It is strong but not very resistant to decay, and is used mainly for general-purpose indoor joinery work. It can be painted, varnished or stained.

Mahogany This is probably the best-known tropical hardwood, and its dark red colour and fine, smooth grain pattern have made it one of the most popular woods for high quality furniture and cabinet-making since it first became commercially available in the late 16th century. The finest wood comes mainly from South America, although the darker African varieties are an acceptable substitute. It is traditionally French-polished, but modern pieces may be varnished.

Oak This is a hardwood widespread across the northern hemisphere, from Europe to Japan and North America. It has a warm mid-brown colour and a coarse

Fig 291 (*above*) Natural timber and man-made boards come in a wide range of sizes. Knowing what to buy helps save waste and money.

grain pattern, with characteristic markings across the grain, and is extremely strong and dense – properties that can make it hard to work. The American and Japanese varieties are generally less strongly marked than European oak.

When still plentiful, oak was widely used for structural elements of buildings (not to mention ships), but its use is nowadays mainly confined to furniture. It is an acidic wood, and so should be joined with brass screw rather than steel ones. It can be stained almost black, or limed to give it a near-silvery finish, but waxing is the best means of enhancing both the colour and grain pattern.

Pine This is a term used to cover a broad group of coniferous softwoods. European redwood is one of the commonest; it is reddish-brown or yellow-brown in colour, straight-grained but fairly resinous, and is widely used for internal joinery and utility furniture. Pitch pine is heavier and darker in colour, and harder to work than redwood, but was popular in the last century for building, flooring and furniture (especially in churches and chapels). Both can be painted, varnished or stained.

Parana pine is the one widely available southern hemisphere softwood, with supplies coming mainly from Brazil. It has an attractive light- to mid-brown colour streaked with red, but its main features are that it is almost knot-free and comes in widths of up to 300mm (12in), making it ideal for shelving and cabinet-making. It is easy to work, but tends to split when nailed. Stain or varnish are the usual finishes.

Ramin This is a bland straight-grained hardwood with a uniform pale red colour, widely used for picture framing and for decorative timber mouldings of all types. It can be stained and varnished.

Sapele This is a tropical hardwood similar in appearance to mahogany but with a very pronounced striped red colour to the grain. It is difficult to plane because of its irregular grain pattern, and is mainly used as a veneer facing on interior doors. Varnish is the best finish to use.

Spruce (or whitewood) This is another of the coniferous softwoods, with a very pale colour and straight, unpronounced grain pattern and an even texture. It is fairly strong but prone to decay, so is mainly used for internal joinery work and is generally painted.

Teak This is one of the most durable (and best-known) tropical hardwoods, and is a dense, strong coarse-grained reddish wood which weathers to an attractive silvery-grey if left unprotected out of doors. It is widely used for furniture-making both as solid wood and in veneer form, but is hard to work and extremely oily, which makes gluing and finishing difficult. It is traditionally oiled to enhance the grain pattern and protect the surface.

Western red cedar This is a light, brownish wood with a very soft texture and a pronounced grain pattern. It is mainly used for outdoor furniture, outbuildings and for wall and roof cladding (with small tile-shaped pieces known as shingles), because a natural oil in the wood makes it extremely resistant to rot and insect attack. It is either left to weather to a silvery grey colour, or is maintained with preservative stains.

Man-Made Boards

Man-made boards are an essential material for every woodworker nowadays. They are versatile, comparatively inexpensive, manufactured to uniform quality (for the most part) and can do a lot of things that natural timber cannot because they are available in big sheets. There are several types, and it pays to know the strengths and weaknesses of each one to get the best out of it.

Blockboard This has a thick core consisting of strips of natural timber; this is sandwiched between outer veneers whose grain runs at right angles to the core grain. More expensive double-faced boards have pairs of surface veneers like plywood, with the outer veneer often of an exotic wood rather than the usual plain birch. It is a relatively dense, strong board, but it can be hard to get the edges neat if the core endgrain is exposed (there are often gaps between the core strips) and making fixings into this edge can be difficult.

Blockboard is graded in the same way as plywood, but the WBP (weather- and boil-proof) grade is not available because the softwood core is not durable enough.

TIMBER SIZES
Softwood is now sold machined to a wide range of standard metric sizes, and the actual cross-sectional sizes are generally about 3mm (⅛in) smaller than the so-called nominal size by which the wood is described.

Standard thicknesses range from 12mm (½in) upwards in 3mm (⅛in) steps up to 25mm (1in), then in 6mm (¼in) steps up to 50mm (2in), in 12mm (½in) steps up to 75mm (3in) and in 25mm (1in) steps thereafter. Standard widths are 12mm (½in), 19mm (¾in), 25mm (1in), 38mm (1½in), 50mm (2in), 75mm (3in), 100mm (4in), 125mm (5in) and 150mm (6in). Wider sections are available to special order.

Hardwood is sold in a far smaller range of sizes, and it is best to ask your supplier what is available when planning a project.

Most suppliers sell wood cut to metric lengths based on the 'unit' of 300mm (12in) – about 5mm (¼in) less than a foot. This means that if you want a piece exactly 5ft (1524mm) long, you will have to buy and cut down the next standard length (1800mm).

Board Materials

Common thicknesses for blockboard are 12, 18 and 25mm (½, ¾ and 1in), although other sizes are less widely available.

Chipboard This is made by binding wood chips together under pressure with synthetic resins to create a rigid, dense and fairly heavy board. It is strong if reasonably well supported, but sawing can leave a crumbly edge (and the resin content quickly blunts saw blades), and screws do not hold well in it. Most grades are not moisture-resistant, and swell alarmingly if they get wet. Various thicknesses are available, from about 6mm (¼in) up to 40mm (1½in), but 12, 18 and 25mm (½, ¾ and 1in) are the commonest.

Standard-grade chipboard has chips of a uniform size, but most boards are the graded-density type with finer chips nearer the surface. The board surface is sanded smooth ready for decorating. Flooring-grade chipboard is denser than other types, and is available with all edges tongued-and-grooved in panels 610mm and 1220mm (2ft and 4ft) wide to match standard joist centres.

Chipboard is also widely available with the board faces and edges covered with natural wood veneers, PVC or melamine coatings (in pastel colours or imitation wood effects), or with plastic laminate. If used for heavy-duty shelving, the supports must be closely spaced to avoid sagging.

Hardboard This is the most widely-used of the fibreboards, and is generally dark brown in colour. Standard hardboard has one smooth face and one with a rough mesh pattern (boards with two smooth faces are known as duo-faced). It is relatively weak, so must be supported by a framework (it is ideal for levelling timber floors), and breaks up if it gets wet. However, it is cheap and will easily bend round curves. The commonest thicknesses are 3, 4 and 6mm (⅛, 3/16 and ¼in).

Tempered hardboard is treated to make it water-resistant, and can be used outdoors. Moulded hardboard has embossed and textured patterns on one face, while decorative hardboards have a PVC or melamine surface which often carries a printed pattern and embossing so it resembles materials such as tongued-and-grooved timber or ceramic tiles. Perforated hardboard is punched with holes (known as pegboard), slots or decorative patterns.

Medium board This is softer and weaker than hardboard, so is usually used in thicker sheets – commonly 13mm (½in). Dense types are used for cladding partitions instead of plasterboard, while softer types are used for pinboards and the like. Both types may be flame-retardant, oil-treated or lacquered. Softboard or insulating board is even less dense than medium board, and as its name implies is generally used for insulating purposes.

Medium-density fibreboard (MDF) This is far stronger than other fibreboards because adhesive is used to bind the fibres together and it is highly compressed so it is much denser than medium board. This gives it the twin advantages of not flaking or splintering when cut, and of giving a clean hard edge which does not need disguising like that of other man-made boards. It is available in thicknesses from around 15mm (⅝in) up to 35mm (1⅜in), and is finding increasingly widespread use in the furniture industry as well as in the home.

Plywood This is made by gluing thin wood veneers together in layers, with the grain in each layer running at right angles to its neighbour to give the board strength and to help resist warping. There are always an odd number of plies, with the grain on the surface plies running parallel with the board's longer edge. Five- and seven-ply boards are the most common, but the thinnest boards may have only three plies.

Birch and gaboon are the commonest timbers used for making plain plywood. This is graded for quality and moisture-resistance. Quality grading refers to the numbers of knots, joins and other surface markings: A is perfect, B is average and BB is suitable only for rough work. The WBP (weather- and boil-proof) grade is suitable for all external uses; MR (moisture-resistant) board is used in damp indoor conditions, and INT for internal work in dry conditions only.

Plywood is also available with a range of exotic surface veneers in woods such as teak, oak and mahogany, or with a decorative plastic surface finish (similar to that of decorative hardboard) for use as wall cladding and the like.

Common board thicknesses are 3, 6, 12 and 19mm (⅛, ¼, ½ and ¾in).

BOARD SIZES
All man-made boards are available in standard 2440 × 1220mm (8 × 4ft) sheets. Many suppliers also sell smaller (and more manageable) sizes – common ones include 1830 × 915mm (6 × 3ft), 1830 × 610mm (6 × 2ft), 1220 × 610mm (4 × 2ft) and 915 × 610mm (3 × 2ft). Some also offer a cut-to-size service, enabling you to order pieces of the precise size you need for a particular project.

Screws and Nails

Screws

The most widely used type of screw is the countersunk screw. This has a head shaped like a truncated cone, so that its flat top finishes flush with the surface of the timber, within a conical recess called a countersink drilled using a countersinking bit. Countersunk screws are made in lengths from 6–150mm (¼–6in) and with either ordinary slotted heads (for use with an ordinary screwdriver) or with one of the cross-head patterns (Phillips, Pozidriv or Supadriv). Depending on the length of the screw you will also have a choice of gauge – the diameter of the screw shank given as a number between 1 and 20; the larger the gauge, the thicker the screw. Nos 8, 10 and 12 gauges are the most widely used in general woodwork.

Other common head types are the raised countersunk, mainly used for fixing hardware to wood when the item has countersunk fixing holes; the round head, used for fixing hardware without countersunk fixing holes; and the pan head, mainly

Fig 292 (*above*) There is a huge range of screws to choose from.

Fig 293 Screw heads may be countersunk, raised countersunk, round or pan-shaped.

Fig 294 The head may have a simple slot, or one of three star shaped recesses – Phillips, Pozidriv or Supadriv.

Fig 295 The screw shank diameter is denoted by its gauge number.

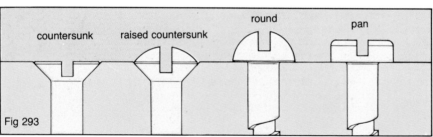

countersunk   raised countersunk   round   pan

Fig 293

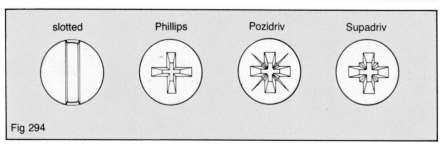

slotted   Phillips   Pozidriv   Supadriv

Fig 294

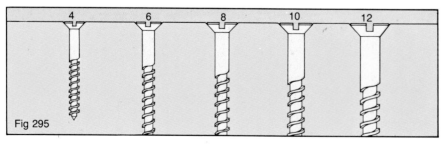

4   6   8   10   12

Fig 295

Pilot and Clearance Holes

Screw gauge	Clearance hole	Pilot hole
4	3mm	bradawl
6	4mm	bradawl
8	5mm	2mm
10	5.5mm	2.5mm
12	6mm	3mm
14	7mm	4mm

used for fixing thin sheet materials. All are found in a more restricted range of sizes than countersunk screws – normally in lengths from 12–50mm (½–2in) and in gauge nos 4 to 10.

Ordinary woodscrews do not grip well in some man-made boards, notably chipboard and the thicker fibreboards. With these materials it is better to use special chipboard screws, which have finer flanges and a shallower pitch to the screw thread so they grip the materials into which they are driven more securely. These screws can of course be used on natural timber too.

Screws such as the Supafast type have a steeper pitch so you need fewer turns to tighten them; they have a thread pattern in the form of a double helix to improve the grip that would otherwise be reduced by the steeper thread pitch. They also have a slightly thinner shank than ordinary screws, which helps to reduce the risk of the wook splitting as the screw is driven in.

Screws come in a variety of materials and finishes. Normal 'self-coloured' steel screws are prone to head damage and will rust, but hardened screws have heads as strong as a screwdriver blade and so will not burr if driven carelessly. Stainless steel or brass screws do not rust, but are expensive. Plating, either BZP (bright zinc plating) or chrome, will prevent rusting for a while; screws with painted (usually black japanned) finishes are generally used for fixing outdoor hardware such as gate hinges and catches.

Screw accessories are used to enhance or conceal the appearance of screwed connections. Brass screw cups – either recessed or surface-mounted – both help provide a better-looking and stronger fixing, by increasing the area bearing down on the wood surface. Screw caps, frequently made of plastic, are used to conceal the screw heads from view, and may be designed for surface fitting (often in conjunction with a washer onto which the screw cap snaps) or for flush or semi-flush use. The latter type is particularly popular with cross-head screws on panel furniture; the cover simply locates in the cross-shaped recess in the screw head.

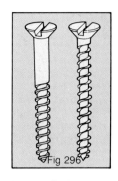

Fig 296 Ordinary wood screws have a smooth shank; chipboard screws are threaded right up to the head.

Fig 297 Metal screw cups.

Fig 298 and 299 Plastic screw caps and covers.

Fig 300 Types of nail.

Nails

These are the commonest types. **Round wire nails (A)** are used for rough carpentry only; 19 to 150mm. **Oval wire nails (B)** are used on general joinery; 25 to 150mm. **Panel pins (C)** are used for fixing thin sheet materials to frameworks and fine work; 15 to 50mm. **Hardboard nails (D)** have diamond-shaped heads that bury themselves in the board surface; 19 to 38mm. **Masonry nails (E)** are hardened nails for fixing things like battens direct to masonry; 15 to 100mm. **Cut floor brads (F)** were traditionally used to fix floorboards; 38 to 75mm. **Cut clasp nails (G)** were used for fixing jobs now usually done by masonry nails; 19 to 30mm. **Round-head nails (H)** are used as an alternative to round wire nails for general carpentry where you want to conceal the nail heads by punching them into the wood; 38 to 75mm. **Plasterboard nails (I)**; 30 to 38mm. **Clout nails (J)** are used for fixing slates and roofing felts; 19 to 100mm. **Tacks (K)** are mainly used for laying carpets; 6 to 30mm. **Upholstery nails (L)**; 3 to 12mm. **Staples (M)** are used for rough carpentry and fixing fencing wires; 10 to 38mm. **Glazing sprigs (N)** secure panes of glass in frames; 12 to 19mm.

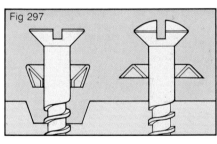

Fig 297

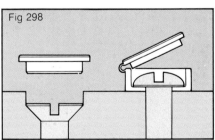

Fig 298

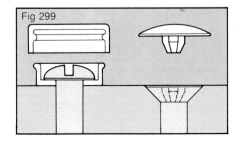

Fig 299

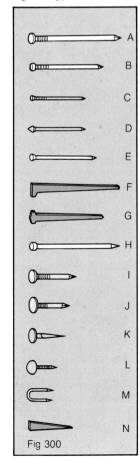

Fig 300

Woodworking Sundries

Abrasives The commonest type is glasspaper, consisting of fine particles of ground glass bonded to a paper backing. It is used primarily for smoothing wood and man-made boards, and comes in nine grades – 3, 2½, S2, M2, F2, 1½, 1, 0 and 00. The finest, 00 grade, is often called flour paper. The standard sheet size is 280 × 230mm (11 × 9in).

Aluminium oxide abrasive is also used for sanding wood, and is the commonest abrasive material for use with power sanders. It comes in disc, belt and sheet form (these are available pre-cut into half-, third- and quarter-sheets to fit orbital sanders of different sizes). The grading system here runs from a coarse grade 3 (also known as grit number 24) to fine 9/0 (number 320).

Silicon carbide paper, better known as wet-and-dry paper, is so called because it can be used wet or dry. It is widely used for rubbing down paintwork, since the paint particles can be washed out periodically to prevent clogging. It is available in thirteen different grades, classified by grit number. Those with grit numbers between 60 and 120 are fairly coarse; 150 to 240 are medium, and 280 to 500 are fine. It comes in sheets the same size as glasspaper.

Adhesives These are used in every branch of do-it-yourself activity, and are immensely useful allies in woodworking. PVA wood adhesive is a white liquid which dries to a clear film, and is ideal for all carpentry work indoors. Out of doors, use a water-proof variety or a two-part powder resin adhesive – usually urea-formaldehyde.

Hinges These come in a wide range of different types, designed to do different jobs. The simplest and most widely used is the butt hinge, consisting of two metal plates which interlock at the hinge knuckle and pivot round a metal pin. Pre-drilled countersunk holes in the plates (known as leaves) allow the hinge to be screwed in place flush with both door and frame. They are generally made from galvanized steel or brass in a range of sizes from 25 to 150mm (1 to 6in) long. Rising butt hinges are a special two-part version, used to swing a room door clear of floor surfaces and also to allow it to be lifted off its hinges if required.

There are many variations on the basic butt hinge principle, designed to hinge things as diverse as table tops, window casements and garden gates.

Lay-on hinges are quite different, having a spring-loaded action designed to pull cabinet doors and the like closed and to allow the door to open beyond 90°. Some are designed for surface-mounting; others have the mechanism housed in a shallow cylinder that is recessed into the inner face of the door.

Fig 301 (*above*) Abrasives come in standard-sized sheets for hand sanding, and in smaller pre-cut sheets for use with orbital sanders.

Fig 302 (*left*) Hinges come in dozens of different patterns, ranging from plain butt hinges for room doors to ornate hinges for cabinets and table tops and the wide opening spring-loaded types widely used on kitchen units.

Woodworking Sundries

Knock-down fittings These are jointing devices widely used on DIY self-assembly furniture to allow the piece to be packed flat and yet to be easily assembled at home. KD fittings, as they soon became known, are now widely available to suit almost any DIY furniture-making project and they provide an excellent alternative to more conventional assembly methods.

The simplest and most widely-used KD fitting is the joint block, which comes in various shapes, sizes and styles. The one-piece block links two components by means of screws driven into them through the block, or may have a lug that is pressed into a hole in one component before a screw is driven into the other. The two-piece block has one piece screwed to each component; then the two blocks are linked by a short bolt.

Cam fittings are two-part fittings which are less obtrusive than blocks because they fit into the thickness of the material, and are so called because they are locked together by turning the shaped locking cam within the fitting. Various types are on the market.

There are several types of screw fittings available, including the well-known Scan fitting where a machine screw passes through one piece into a threaded dowel set in the other. Screw-in brass dowels give the joint extra strength. Other types include the bolt and screw socket, the bolt and tee nut, the hanger bolt and the connecting bolt with its brass heads.

Some of these will join things like kitchen units together side by side, but you can use a special cabinet connector screw instead for the neatest finish. There is also a special screw used to butt-join lengths of worktop.

Wallplugs These small fixing devices that allow screws to be driven into masonry when fixing things to walls. The most common is a plastic plug that expands widthways in its pre-drilled hole as the screw is driven; many have a flange that prevents the plug from disappearing into the hole, and have barbed 'teeth' that grip the hole sides to help provide a firm fixing. They are usually sold moulded on 'trees', and come in a range of sizes; one size will usually make a satisfactory fixing with the commonest screw sizes (gauge nos 8, 10 and 12), but it is best to follow the manufacturer's recommendations as far as screw and masonry drill size are concerned.

For making heavier-duty fixings into walls, expansion anchors or masonry bolts with metal sleeves are used instead. These require a deeper, wider hole but provide an extremely strong fixing. They should be set into the centre of bricks and blocks, not into the mortar courses between them. They come complete with a threaded screw or bolt, and are available with hook and eye bolts as well as the more conventional hexagonal heads.

For making fixings to hollow walls and ceilings, a range of expanding anchors and toggles is available. Toggles have either a drop-down bar (gravity type) or spring-loaded wings which are pushed through the hole to grop the inner face of the wallboard; the toggle is lost if the fixing screw is withdrawn. Expanding anchors have plastic or rubber collars which are compressed against the inner face of the wall as the fixing screw is driven, and remain in place if it is withdrawn.

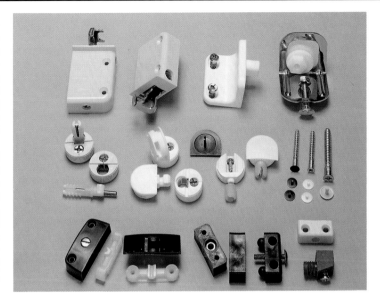

Fig 303 (*above*) Knock-down fittings have revolutionized the assembly of furniture of all types, making it easy to put things together sturdily without the need for traditional jointing techniques.

Fig 304 (*left*) Fixing devices are essential for holding screws in solid and hollow walls and in ceilings. There's one for every situation.

Glossary

Architrave Decorative or plain moulding used to frame door or window openings.

Arris rail Triangular-shaped horizontal rail fixed between fence posts to carry the vertical boards in a weatherboard fence.

Baluster One of the vertical posts fitted between a staircase's string and its hand-rail to form a balustrade.

Batten Length of timber fixed to a wall to provide support (as for the end of a shelf) or a fixing ground (for cladding).

Bevel An angled edge to a piece of timber, not at 90° to its neighbours.

Bridle joint A joint formed with a tenon or a pair of wide housings cut on one component fitting into an open slot cut in the end of the other.

Butt joint A joint formed between two components without overlapping.

Casement The side-hung or top-hung light of a hinged window.

Chamfer A bevel cut at 45° to the edge of the timber.

Countersink A cone-shaped recess drilled in a surface (usually in wood) to accept the head of a countersunk screw.

Cylinder lock A surface-mounted lock with the lock mechanism set in a hole drilled through the door stile.

Dado A wooden moulding fixed round a room at waist height to protect the walls from damage by furniture.

Dowel joint A butt joint which is re-inforced by dowels fixed into the mating surfaces along the joint line.

Endgrain The surface exposed when wood is cut across the grain direction.

Flush door A door with flat faces, usually formed with man-made boards fixed to both sides of a timber frame.

Grain The direction of the wood fibres, parallel with the tree's line of growth.

Halving joint A joint formed when half the thickness of each overlapping component is cut away.

Head plate The top member of a stud partition wall, fixed to the ceiling.

Housing joint A joint formed with the end of one component fitting into a slot cut in the other, often used for shelves.

KD fitting Abbreviation for knock-down fitting, a mechanical corner joint that can be quickly assembled or dismantled.

Lap joint A joint formed when one component is laid on top of another and then fixed to it.

Light A fixed window pane, a hinged casement or a sash.

Mitre joint A butt joint formed between two components with ends cut at 45°.

Mortise-and-tenon joint A joint formed with a tenon cut on one piece fitting into an enclosed slot (the mortise) in the other.

Mortise lock A recessed lock, fitted into a mortise in the door edge.

Moulding Timber machined into a decorative cross-section, such as an architrave or picture rail.

Mullion A vertical member subdividing a window frame into individual lights.

Muntin The central vertical member of a panel door, separating the panels.

Newel post One of the main vertical structural members of a timber staircase, supporting the strings and handrails.

Nogging A short horizontal timber fixed between the vertical studs of a stud partition wall.

Nosing The front edge of a stair tread.

Panel door A framed door with the spaces between the stiles, rails and muntins filled with thinner panels.

Parting bead Slim moulding separating the channels in which sashes slide.

Picture rail A wooden moulding fixed round a room at head height to support pictures.

Rail A horizontal frame member.

Riser The vertical face of a step.

Sash A sliding light in a sash window.

Scribing Marking and shaping one surface so it is a snug fit to an uneven one.

Skirting A wooden moulding fitted round a room at floor level to protect the wall plaster from accidental damage.

Sole plate The bottom member of a stud partition wall, fixed to the floor.

Staff bead A slim moulding holding the inner sash of a sash window in its frame.

Stile The vertical side member of a panel door, casement or sash.

String The sloping board at each side of a staircase, supporting the ends of the treads and risers.

Stud A full-height vertical member of a stud partition wall.

Tenon The end of a frame component reduced in cross-section to fit into a mortise or open slot cut in another component.

Tongued-and-grooved boards Boards with a tongue cut on one edge and a groove on the other, allowing the two to interlock when butt-jointed edge to edge.

Transom A horizontal member subdividing a window frame.

Tread The horizontal face of a step.

USEFUL ADDRESSES

Information on timber and timber products

British Woodworking Federation,
82 New Cavendish St.
London W1M 8AD
Tel: 071–580 5588

Chipboard Promotion Association,
50 Station Road,
Marlow,
Buckinghamshire
SL7 1NN
Tel: 06284 3022

Fibre Building Board Development Organisation,
1 Hanworth Road,
Feltham,
Middlesex TW13 5AF
Tel: 081–751 6107

Timber Research and Development Association,
Chiltern House,
Stocking Lane,
Hughenden Valley,
High Wycombe,
Buckinghamshire
HP14 4ND
Tel: 024024 3091

Specialists for major projects

Federation of Master Builders,
14 Great James Street,
London WC1
Tel: 071–242 7583

Glass and Glazing Federation,
44–48 Borough High St,
London SE1 1XB
Tel: 071–403 7177

Index

Index